Edward Hyde, Earl of Clarendon

Twayne's English Authors Series

Arthur F. Kinney, Editor
University of Massachusetts, Amherst

TEAS 337

EDWARD HYDE
(1609-1674)
Courtesy of National Portrait Gallery, London.

Edward Hyde, Earl of Clarendon

By George E. Miller

University of Delaware

Twayne Publishers • *Boston*

Edward Hyde, Earl of Clarendon

George E. Miller

Copyright © 1983 by G. K. Hall & Company
All Rights Reserved
Published by Twayne Publishers
A Division of G. K. Hall & Company
70 Lincoln Street
Boston, Massachusetts 02111

Book Production by John Amburg
Book Design by Barbara Anderson

Printed on permanent/durable acid-
free paper and bound in The United
States of America.

Library of Congress Cataloging in Publication Data

Miller, George.
  Edward Hyde, Earl of Clarendon.

  (Twayne's English authors series ;
  TEAS 337)
  Bibliography: p. 156
  Includes index.
  1. Clarendon, Edward Hyde, Earl of, 1609-1674.
2. Great Britain—History—Puritan Revolution, 1642-1660.
3. Clarendon, Edward Hyde, Earl, of, 1609-1674.
I. Title.   II. Series.
DA400.C63M54   1983   941.06'0924 [B]   82-15613
ISBN 0-8057-6823-8

For Craig, his book

Contents

About the Author

George E. Miller received the B.A. (1964) and M.A. (1966) in English from The Pennsylvania State University and the Ph.D. (1969) in English from the University of Connecticut. A specialist in Milton and seventeenth-century literature, he has published numerous articles, and is, as well, the author or coauthor of five books. He has been a research fellow at the Folger Shakespeare Library (1973). He is presently Professor of English at the University of Delaware and Director, Lower-Division Programs in English.

Editor's Foreword

The monumental *History* of England in the seventeenth century by Edward Hyde, Earl of Clarendon, is the first in a tradition of literary works that will include those by Gibbon and Macaulay. George E. Miller's study of Hyde unscrambles the three separate drafts of his account, demonstrates how Hyde added and later deleted autobiography to turn history into a personal defense of his own political activity as a royalist, and analyzes the final literary form Hyde created which is at once personal and impersonal, factual and creative. In detailing Hyde's own career as chief advisor to Charles I and Charles II, Miller also examines Hyde's statements on religion and his famous reply to Hobbes's *Leviathan* in light of his literary precedents. Finally, Miller shows how Hyde's interest in character portraiture and the classical theory of history as the decisions and actions of men utilized such models as Theophrastus and Joseph Hall to change the shape of contemporary history. This is a valuable summary of the many contributions of the Earl of Clarendon to English literature.

Arthur F. Kinney

Preface

Edward Hyde, Earl of Clarendon, was one of the most prominent political figures in seventeenth-century England. Advisor to
Charles I, architect of the Restoration settlement, and Lord Chancellor under Charles II, Clarendon was in an unique position to
record the history of the English civil war years. He did so in his
massive *History of the Rebellion and Civil Wars in England*, a
work which established a tradition of English historical writing
which would later include writers such as Edward Gibbon, Thomas
Carlyle, and Thomas Babington Macaulay. This book is intended as
an introduction to Clarendon's *History*. The first four chapters,
which form the core of this study, analyze the *History* from four
different points of view. Since Clarendon's interpretation of the
events of the war is a reflection of his attitudes toward politics as a
practical science and religion as a political force, the study concludes
with two chapters which examine three of his minor works on
politics and religion.

Clarendon did not just record the history of his time; he played a
vital role in making it. The daily demands of administration left
him little time for literary labors. He wrote only when circumstances prevented him from participating. And when he did write,
it was always about the political events of his age and the part that
he played in them. Since his life is such an integral part of his
writing and since it inevitably shapes and colors his attitudes, I have
devoted chapter 1 to a background sketch of the crucial years of
Clarendon's political life.

The *History* is composed of material written at three different
times over a twenty-five-year period. When it was finished in
1671–72, Clarendon combined a manuscript "History," written in
1646–48, with a manuscript "Life," written in 1668–71, adding
some material as he went. Questions of structure, selectivity, and
purpose in the final *History* are, correspondingly, difficult to
answer. Chapter 2 is an examination of the *History* as it evolved
through its three stages of composition.

Despite its patchwork nature, the *History* emerges as a unified work. Chapters 3 and 4 examine the *History* as a whole—first, as an historical work and, second, as a literary work. Chapter 3 places the *History* in the context of historical writing running from the classical historians to the Renaissance historians Machiavelli and Davila. It analyzes as well Clarendon's view of the purpose of history, of historical causation; it concludes with an examination of his use of source material in compiling the *History*. Chapter 4 examines the links between history and literature and offers an analysis of three elements of fiction—plot, character, and narrative voice—in the *History*. The one aspect of the *History* which has long been singled out for particular praise—the "character sketches"—is examined at length in chapter 5.

In the final two chapters, I treat at some length three minor books. I have done so because they significantly broaden our understanding of Clarendon's attitudes toward politics and religion. Space limitations preclude any treatment of the other minor works or of Clarendon's pamphleteering efforts on behalf of two kings. In the first chapter and in the bibliography, I have at least identified those significant items which are not covered here.

The debts which one amasses in such a study cannot be adequately acknowledged. Like everyone who writes about Clarendon, I owe much to the work of Sir Charles Firth and the Reverend B. H. G. Wormald. I am indebted to Professor David Berkowitz of Brandeis University for several helpful suggestions at a point at which they were particularly needed; to Professor Tai Liu of the University of Delaware and to Professor Joan Hartman of the College of Staten Island, CUNY, for their criticisms and suggestions on an earlier draft of this book; and most especially to Professor Arthur F. Kinney of the University of Massachusetts for his extensive help in reshaping this study. As always, I must acknowledge the help of my secretary, Deborah Lyall. Finally, the patience, understanding, and suggestions of my wife, Rachel, have sustained and helped me throughout.

I am particularly grateful to Dr. O. B. Hardison and the Trustees of the Folger Shakespeare Library for a short-term fellowship. The helpfulness and hospitality of the staff make research seem a noble task. A University of Delaware summer research grant enabled me to complete a draft of the study. The research for the book was done at a number of libraries both in the United States and England, but special thanks must be given to the staff of Duke Humfrey's Reading Room, Bodleian Library, Oxford University.

Finally, I thank the Delegates of the Clarendon Press, Oxford, for permission to quote from Clarendon's work.

George E. Miller

University of Delaware

Chronology

1646-1648	Begins work on the original "History of the Rebellion."
1648	26 June, leaves Jersey to rejoin the Prince.
1649	30 January, execution of Charles I; 26 November, arrives in Madrid on the Spanish embassy.
1650	24 June, Charles II arrives in Scotland.
1651	March, leaves Spain; December, rejoins the king in Paris.
1658	13 January, becomes Lord Chancellor.
1660	14 April, Charles II's Declaration of Breda; 29 May, Charles II enters London; 27 October, elected Chancellor of Oxford; 3 November, raised to peerage as Baron Hyde of Hindon.
1661	20 April, created Viscount Cornbury and Earl of Clarendon.
1662	May, Charles II marries Catherine of Braganza; October, sale of Dunkirk to France.
1665	February, second Anglo-Dutch War is declared.
1667	June, naval disaster in the Medway; July, peace concluded for the war; November, impeached and flees England.
1668-1671	Lives in Montpellier.
1668	July, begins the "Life."
1670	August, "Life" is completed in manuscript.
1671-1674	Lives in Moulins.
1671	June, his son Laurence visits, bringing the manuscript of the original "History."
1671-1672	"The History of the Rebellion" is finished.
1674	Publication of *Animadversions*; December, moves to Rouen, where he dies on 9 December.

1675   4 January, his body is buried in Westminster Abbey.

1676   Publication of *A Brief View and Survey*.

1702-1704   Publication of the first edition of *The History of the Rebellion*.

Chapter One
Clarendon's Life and Times

Member of Parliament, advisor to Charles I, propagandist for the royalist cause, architect of the Restoration settlement, Lord Chancellor and chief minister under Charles II, Edward Hyde, Earl of Clarendon, was one of the most prominent royalists in seventeenth-century England. As a monument and record of his roles during those turbulent years, he collected a massive quantity of state papers, correspondence, documents—some 100 folio volumes in the Bodleian Library, Oxford, the chief repository of his papers. He left, as well, an autobiography, *The Life of Edward Hyde, Earl of Clarendon.* Yet among all of those papers and records, little survives that relates in any way to his private life. As Thomas H. Lister, his first biographer, noted: "The biography of Clarendon must be essentially that of a public man. Few, brief, and unimportant are the extant passages which exhibit him in domestic life. Either he wrote little on private matters, or letters on such subjects were deemed unworthy to be preserved."[1] Even his autobiography reflects this disparity, for Clarendon records his birth and childhood in one paragraph, his education at Oxford in another, and his role in the first session of the Long Parliament in over fifty pages.

There is little in Edward Hyde's early life that presages the prominent part he would come to play in English history. He was born at Dinton in Wiltshire on 18 February 1609, the third son of Henry Hyde and Mary Langford. His father, an M.A. graduate from Oxford, educated for the law at Middle Temple, was a country gentleman. Edward's early schooling was provided by the parish vicar and his father. He was admitted to Magdalen Hall, Oxford, in 1622 at the age of fourteen and graduated B.A. on 14 February 1626. Originally destined to enter the Church, the death of his elder brother made him the sole surviving son, and he entered Middle Temple in 1625 to study law; he was called to the bar on 22 November 1633.

Even as he "betook himself to business," as he later remarked in his *Life*, Hyde was always careful to cultivate "polite" learning and a wide circle of distinguished and influential friends. These included poets Ben Jonson, Thomas Carew, and Edmund Waller; historians John Selden and Thomas May; classicist John Hales and theologian William Chillingworth; ecclesiastics Gilbert Sheldon, George Morley, and John Earle; and a wide variety of politically and socially prominent men.

Hyde's position was further enhanced by his two marriages. In 1629 he married Anne Ayliffe, the daughter of Sir George Ayliffe, of Gretenham, Wiltshire. The marriage connected him with the Villiers family, the most prominent member of which was George Villiers, Duke of Buckingham, favorite of James I. Anne died within six months and Hyde remarried some four years later on 10 July 1634. His new wife was Frances Aylesbury, whose father Sir Thomas Aylesbury was master of the mint and a judge. Apparently because of his new connection, Hyde was appointed keeper of the writs and rolls of common pleas in December 1634. Hyde's fortunes were further improved through the influence of Archbishop Laud, who had been impressed with Hyde's actions on behalf of some London merchants.

Member of Parliament

With the opening of the Short Parliament on 13 April 1640, Hyde, chosen from Wootton Bassett, Wiltshire, began his political career. From the very outset, his actions marked him as a critic of Charles's government. Like many members of that Parliament, he was disturbed by a number of abuses in the administration of law which had occurred during the period 1628–40, the years in which Charles I had summoned no parliament: at the opening of the Short Parliament, Hyde specifically protested against the Earl Marshal's Court. Its jurisdiction was confined to cases involving disparaging remarks made about members of the nobility. This court, Hyde asserted, was "without colour or shadow of law" (*Life*, 1:78). Thomas Lister, Hyde's biographer, notes that this protest was "the first motion in this parliament having for its object the redress of a specific grievance."[2] The Short Parliament had hardly begun its work when Charles, angry that the members wanted only to discuss their grievances against his government instead of acting to grant his request for money, dissolved it on 5 May 1640.

The disasters of the Second Scots' War forced Charles to summon another Parliament, which opened on 3 November of that same year. Hyde was returned—this time for Saltash, Cornwall—and continued his attack upon the abuses in the administration of law, renewing his attack on the Earl Marshal's Court. He got a committee appointed, of which he was chairman, to investigate it. "The very entrance upon this inquisition," he notes, "put an end to that upstart court, which never presumed to sit afterwards; and so that grievance was thoroughly abolished" (*Life*, 1:84). He also served on a number of other committees including several which involved strengthening and enforcing the persecution of Papists. In addition, he was chairman of the committee which examined the illegality of the Council of the North, often called the Court of York; another which was concerned with the jurisdiction of the Lord President and Council of the Marches and Wales; and a third which "examined the miscarriages of the judges, in the case of ship-money, and in other cases of judicatory, in their several courts; and prepared charges thereupon against them" (*Life*, 1:86). On 26 April 1641 he delivered a speech against the Court of York at a conference of both Houses.[3] Later, on 6 July he preferred charges against the Barons of the Exchequer before a conference of both Houses.[4] Despite the rather sympathetic treatment of Strafford in the *History*, Hyde actively supported his impeachment and was involved in a series of committees helping to collect evidence against Strafford and to expedite his trial. Apparently, Hyde voted for the bill of attainder.

On the basis of his activity in the Short Parliament and in the first session of the Long Parliament, Hyde was, as B. H. G. Wormald notes, "an enemy from the royal standpoint."[5] He had been instrumental in checking the king's use of direct judical power through the prerogative courts. On 5 July 1641, the king passed the bills abolishing the Court of Star Chamber and the Court of High Commission. On 7 August he passed the bill which annulled all the proceedings relating to ship-money. Yet in his *History*, Hyde laments the destruction of these instruments as an infringement of royal prerogative. The original bill on the Star Chamber, he writes, was designed to "limit and regulate the proceedings of that court," not to abolish it. The alteration in that bill was a result of actions by the "violent party," that is, the opposition led by Pym. The Court was a "great branch of the prerogative" and "whilst it was gravely and moderately governed was an excellent expedient to preserve the dignity of the King, the honor of his Council, and the peace and security of the kingdom" (3:264). Similarly, the Court of High Commission, while it had much "overflowed the banks which should have contained it, not only in meddling with things that in truth were not properly within their conusance," still, when "exercised with moderation," was "an excellent means to vindicate and preserve the dignity and peace of the Church (3:257, 258).

It can be argued that such observations, written five to six years after Hyde's participation, might not represent his original attitudes, that he might be apologizing for the part that he had played then. Nevertheless, the limited knowledge that we do have about Hyde's position in the early 1640s argues for the sincerity of his later remarks. The point is simply that we should be wary of regarding Hyde's position in the first session of the Long Parliament as advocating the destruction of all the instruments of prerogative rule. For Hyde, reformation, that is, confining the scope of the jurisdiction of such instruments to their original legal basis, would have sufficed. In this sense Hyde appears as a constitutional royalist from the outset of his political career.

He was not, however, willing to agree to any substantial alteration in ecclesiastical matters. In February 1641 he opposed receiving the London petition calling for the abolition of episcopacy; in May, the demands of the Scots for the unity of religion. He also spoke against the bill to take away the bishops' votes in Parliament on 30 March, arguing on constitutional grounds that "it was changing the whole frame and constitution of the kingdom, and of the Parliament itself" (3:150). In the hopes of preventing him from obstructing the passage of the Root and Branch Bill, he was made chairman of the committee where he was, nevertheless, able to force the bill's discontinuance. As a result of his efforts on behalf of episcopacy, the king sent for him and, Hyde records, "took notice of his affection to the church, for which, he said, 'he thanked him more than for all the rest'" (*Life*, 1:93). This interview took place sometime shortly before the king began his journey to Scotland in August 1641. On 9 September, the first session of the Long Parliament recessed until 20 October.

If Hyde's efforts in the first session had been predominantly directed toward securing the correction of just constitutional grievances against the king's arbitrary and illegal use of prerogative rule, his efforts in the second session were directed toward an attempt to check an equally dangerous drift in the other direction—toward the constitutionally unjustifiable powers which were gradually claimed and assumed by Parliament. Hyde began to play a "mediating" role between the two forces, but since the initiative had fallen to Pym, it inevitably meant that Hyde was increasingly forced to defend the king's interests. He attacked, for example, a motion that Commons have a negative voice in the choice of councillors for the king. Sir Simonds D'Ewes records that Hyde replied that the king's councillors were his own business and considering that the king had passed the bills abolishing the Court of Star Chamber, the Court of High Commission, and ship-money, "all particulars were in a good condition if we could but preserve them as they were."[6] D'Ewes also notes that Hyde was the first to object to Pym's Additional Instruction to the parliamentary committee attending the king in Scotland that aid for suppressing the Irish rebellion be dependent upon the removal of "evil" councillors about the king and Parliament's approval of new appointments.[7]

Hyde's major effort in this session, however, was his opposition to the Grand Remonstrance. In the first session, a committee was appointed to prepare a Remonstrance on the State of the Kingdom setting forth the various grievances which Parliament had against the king. The committee had never made a report to the House, but now, Pym sought to have it presented, passed, and published before the king's return from Scotland. Hyde led the opposition against the Remonstrance, but it was eventually carried by eleven votes in a thin house in the early hours of the morning. He also was able to

keep the Remonstrance from being published but it was presented
to the king. Later, when the Commons approved a motion to
publish the document, Hyde "only to give vent to his own indignation, and without the least purpose of communicating it" (*Life*, 2:1)
prepared an answer. This document was accidentally discovered by
Lord Digby, who, with the weight of the king's personal request,
persuaded Hyde to allow it to be published as the king's "official"
answer.[8] This was the first of many declarations and pamphlets
which Hyde would write for Charles.

Advisor to Charles I

In January 1642 Charles called Falkland and Culpepper to his
Privy Council, making Falkland Secretary of State in place of Vane,
and Culpepper Chancellor of the Exchequer in place of Cottington.
Both appointments were probably suggested by Hyde. At the same
time, the king offered to make Hyde Solicitor General in place of St.
John. Hyde declined, arguing that he could best serve the king
privately. Falkland, Culpepper, and Hyde were to be responsible
for conducting the king's affairs in Parliament and giving him
"constant advice what he was to do, without which, he declared
again very solemnly, he would make no step in the parliament"
(*Life*, 2:5). Charles was not good to his word and apparently with
the encouragement of Lord Digby allowed the introduction of the
bishops' petition in the House of Lords. The bishops, who had been
prevented from taking their seats in the House of Lords by the
hostile crowds, protested that all proceedings in the House since
their absence were "null and of none effect." This impolitic and
unparliamentary dissent resulted in their impeachment and so
their exclusion from giving any assistance to the king's cause in
Parliament. Digby also was principally responsible for Charles's
attempt to seize the five members of the Commons. As Wormald
has pointed out, this move was "the culmination of a succession of
impolitic and foolish actions, the effect of which was to submerge
Hyde's attempted new departure in pacification in an access of
confusion and mistrust unparalleled up to that moment."[9] Both
actions had been undertaken without the advice of the three and
contrary to the king's promise.

The three men continued, however, their efforts for the king. His blunders, which led to his withdrawal from London to Hampton Court, had placed the three advisors in an increasingly awkward position in the House. We know very little about the extent of Hyde's influence upon the king during this time. He writes that he was opposed to both the bishops' Exclusion Bill, which the king signed on Culpepper's advice, and to the ordinance for the settlement of the militia, which the king did not sign (*Life*, 2:18). The king was stalling for time until the queen, carrying the crown jewels, could safely sail from England. He ordered the Prince of Wales to move to Greenwich to meet him, and Parliament, fearing the worst, appointed three members, one lord and two commoners, to carry their objections to the king. One of the commoners was Hyde. On 25 February 1642 they met the king at Canterbury where they delivered their message and received the king's sharp reply. Hyde visited the king that night and persuaded him that such an answer could only damage his position. In its place, Hyde, Falkland, and Culpepper drafted a more moderate statement. On 27 February, at Greenwich, Hyde had his second long private interview with Charles. It was at this meeting that Charles asked him to "prepare and send him answers to such declarations or messages as the parliament should send to him." The significance of Hyde's new role is noted by S. R. Gardiner:

Charles's acceptance of Hyde as his unofficial adviser marks a new departure in the constitutional system of the English monarchy. Hyde's great achievement was to throw over the doctrine which Strafford had inherited from the Tudors, which taught that there was a prerogative above the law, capable of developing out of itself special and transcendent powers to meet each emergency as it arose, whether Parliament approved or not. The King, according to Hyde, was to work in combination with his Parliament; but he was not to allow the House of Commons to force its will upon the House of Lords, still less was he to allow both Houses combined to compel him to give the Royal assent to Bills of which his conscience disapproved.[10]

Hyde, in his *History*, defined the position he now created for the king: "The King's resolution was to shelter himself wholly under the law, to grant any thing that by the law he was obliged to grant, and to deny what by the law was in his own power and which he found inconvenient to consent to, and to oppose and punish any extravagant attempt by the force and power of the law; presuming that the King and the law together would have been strong enough for any encounter that could happen"(5:12). Gardiner is critical of the negative nature of the position: "that such a conception of the constitution could under any circumstances have been permanently adopted is absolutely impossible."[11] There is no reason, however, to assume that Hyde ever envisioned the strategy as anything other than a temporary measure. Pym's success in the House was, in large part, related to the king's continued blunders. If Hyde could force the king to retreat into a constitutionally justifiable position and then stay there, it might be possible to deprive Pym of the support of the more moderate members of the Commons. The success of such a plan depended, however, on a passive and peaceful king, and Charles was neither. The king moved north, planning to seize Hull, a seaport through which he could receive whatever aid the queen secured from abroad.

From the end of February through May 1642, Hyde stayed in London and wrote answers, apparently with at least the advice of Falkland and Culpepper, to the messages and declarations of Parliament. The texts or summaries of the most important of these appear in the *History*. Hyde was a successful propagandist, though there is little doubt that he sincerely believed that his arguments would contribute to a peaceful settlement. Ironically, he was unable to dissuade Parliament from widening the breach, while enabling Charles to create a substantial enough base of support for him to wage war. Through these papers, Hyde notes in the *History*, the king "had not only to a degree wound himself out of that labyrinth in which four months before they [Parliament] had involved him with their privileges, fears, and jealousies, but had even so well informed the people that they began to question both their logic and their law ... and that they were not only denied by the King what they required, but that the King's reasons for his denial made very many conclude the unreasonableness of their demands" (5:150).

It became increasingly dangerous for Hyde to sit in Parliament. Culpepper had discovered a plan to impeach the three advisors while they all attended the House and they arranged, in turn, never to be present together in Parliament (*Life*, 2:39–40). Later, in May 1642, Hyde received a letter from the king directing him to come as soon as possible to York. Hyde delayed his departure until after Parliament issued the Declaration of 19 May. Taking this document with him in order to prepare an answer, Hyde left London after informing Parliament that his ill health necessitated some country air. He eventually joined the king at York in early June.

Throughout the period in which he was with the king, from June 1642 until his departure with the Prince of Wales in March 1645, Hyde was responsible for almost all of the king's official statements and declarations. The only two important exceptions are the answer to the Nineteen Propositions, written by Falkland and Culpepper (*Life*, 2:61–62) and part of the king's declaration concerning the attack on Brentford, 12 November 1642, which was written by Falkland (*History*, 6:note to 126). In his *Life*, Hyde records that he also wrote a number of occasional pieces for the king, but only one of these is attributed to Hyde, and that on the basis of his own statement (2:70).[12]

In addition to the paper war which Hyde conducted for the king, his other services for the royal cause during the wars were largely confined to administrative and financial matters. He was present at the first battle of the war at Edgehill, but that seems to have been the extent of his military experience. The rest of those years, from October 1642 to March 1645, he lived in All Souls College, Oxford. Even after his flight from Parliament, his status within Charles's government remained unofficial, but this was largely because of Hyde's own reservations. In his *Life* he proudly quotes a letter from Charles to his queen: "I must make Ned Hyde secretary of state, for the truth is, I can trust nobody else" (2:73). Hyde refused, but later accepted the position of Chancellor of the Exchequer after Culpepper had been promoted to Master of the Rolls. On 22 February 1643, he was made a member of the Privy Council and knighted. The king's council in Oxford consisted of seventeen members; another nine had refused to follow the king, choosing to stay with

Parliament. Policy, however, was discussed by a "junto" composed of Hyde and five other councillors who met every Friday at Oriel College.

Hyde and the "junto" had very little influence on the conduct of the war and there was considerable friction between the king's civilian advisors and his military commanders. Throughout the period, Hyde's efforts were consistently directed toward negotiating a peace settlement. He played an active role in the Treaty of Oxford in the spring of 1644, where he again pursued the possibility of appointing influential members of the Parliamentary opposition to places of trust and power within Charles's government. It was Hyde who, after the Scots accepted Parliament's invitation to invade England, was responsible for the letter sent from the royalist peers to the Council of State in Scotland. The strategy was to demonstrate that the Long Parliament was no longer a representative body and that a substantial majority of the upper house supported the king. A similar attempt to convince the people that Parliament was now neither representative nor free led to the Oxford Parliament. The king wanted to dissolve the Long Parliament, but Hyde pointed out the constitutional dangers and the fruitlessness of such an attempt. Instead, he proposed that the king summon the members of Parliament to meet in Oxford, January 1644. While the Oxford Parliament did lend an appearance of legality to some of the king's efforts to raise money, it proved ineffective in its peace-seeking attempts. Even long after any real hope for a negotiated peace had passed, Hyde continued his efforts. At the Treaty of Uxbridge in January 1645, he was the king's principal spokesman and negotiator and responsible for preparing all the written papers representing the royalist position.[13]

Advisor to the Prince of Wales

After the failure of the Treaty of Uxbridge and with the increasingly gloomy military situation, the king decided that he and the Prince of Wales must separate. The initial plan was for the Prince to move to the West, where he might be able to settle some of the dissensions which plagued the king's forces there. Moreover, should it be necesssary, the West was the only area from which the

Prince could easily and safely flee the country. To accompany the fourteen-year-old boy, Charles appointed a council which included both Culpepper and Hyde. With great reluctance, Hyde separated from Charles on 4 March 1645 and started for Bristol with the Prince. The military situation in the West was totally chaotic, in part because of the inadequacies of and the hostilities between the principal military commanders. During the next year, the prince and his civilian council tried in vain to resolve the basic problems of administration and command. Lord Hopton, also a member of the prince's council, finally assumed command in January 1646, but by then the king's forces in the West were rapidly dissolving. With the defeat of Hopton's forces at Torrington, 16 February 1646, the royalist army totally collapsed and it became imperative that the prince leave England. On 2 March the prince and his small retinue sailed for Scilly, arriving on 4 March. Parliament summoned the prince to surrender, sending a small fleet to enforce their will. The prince, however, escaped to the greater security of Jersey, arriving there 17 April 1646.

The queen immediately urged that the prince join her in France. Hyde, in particular, adamantly opposed such an idea until such time as it was absolutely necessary. The queen prevailed, and in July 1646, the prince left Jersey. For nearly two years, Hyde remained on the island. Removed from any direct role in the political events of the period, he turned to his books and to writing. He had begun his original "History" on 18 March 1646 while still on Scilly; and by the time that he left Jersey on 26 June 1648 he had completed his narrative to the beginning of the campaign of 1644. In his *Life* he wrote that during his stay on Jersey between his books and his "papers" he "seldom spent less than ten hours in the day" (5:5). Much of his reading was in the work of other historians. He read widely in Thucydides, Livy, Tacitus, Plutarch, and other such works as Josepheus's *The History of the Jews*, Grotius's *De Jure Belli et Pacis*, and Camden's *Britannia*. [14] He also maintained a voluminous correspondence with his friends which is a particularly valuable index to his understanding of the political events in England.

In addition, he worked on several other manuscripts during this same period. On 29 June 1646 he began an account of the western

campaign from 1645 through the spring of 1646, a vindication of
the part played by the Prince's civilian council. This manuscript, a
copy of which was endorsed by Hyde "Concerning the westerne
businesse," was eventually revised and included in the *History*.
Another short fragment, a narrative of the relations between the
prince's council and the Duke of Hamilton, who was imprisoned in
Pendennis Castle, was begun in September 1646. This was also
revised and included in the *History*. Both manuscripts are essentially defenses of Hyde's part in the western "business" rather than
royalist propaganda. Hyde did, however, contribute one final pamphlet to the king's cause. The House of Commons, on 17 January
1648, had published a declaration explaining the reasons for their
earlier vote of No Further Addresses to the king. As soon as he
received a copy in Jersey, Hyde wrote an answer which was sent to
England and published on 3 May.[15] On 28 July, a second and much
longer edition, again the work of Hyde, was published under a
slightly different title.[16] Finally, it was on Jersey that he began work
on his series of reflections upon the Psalms, a work to which he
returned during his embassy to Spain in 1650 and again during his
final exile in 1668.

Advisor to Charles II

With the outbreak of the second civil war, Hyde was summoned
by the queen to join the prince in France. The prospect of another
war necessitated experienced advisors for the young prince. On 26
June 1648 Hyde left Jersey, although it was September before he
was reunited with the prince. His immediate efforts were directed
toward the pragmatic problem of finding money to support the
prince's court. After the execution of Charles, Scotland had proclaimed Charles II King of Scotland and sent commissioners to
invite him there. The proclamation, however, was conditional
upon his acceptance of the Covenant. The king preferred to go to
Ireland, where prospects looked good for some substantial support
for his restoration.

But Lord Cottington took this opportunity to propose an
embassy to Spain. Its purpose was to obtain financial aid from the
Spanish king and his assistance in negotiating a settlement of the

hostilities in Ireland. Cottington asked Hyde to accompany him, and Hyde, weary of the "continual contentions and animosity" which plagued the court, agreed. They left Paris on 29 September 1649, arriving in Madrid on 26 November. The Spanish king, however, like all the kings of Christendom, was unreceptive, and made it clear that Charles was to expect no assistance or intervention. The ambassadors stayed, expecting to hear from Charles after his arrival in Ireland, but with the appointment of Cromwell as Lord Lieutenant of Ireland and with his quick series of military successes there, any thought of Charles's going to Ireland was laid aside. The Scottish commissioners continued to press their request for the king to come to Scotland, and in June 1650 Charles sailed, leaving his servants and chaplains behind. There was nothing for Hyde to do but continue on in Spain.

During this interval, he turned to reading and writing. Here he began collecting materials for his history of the papal succession and continued work on "Contemplations and Reflexions Upon the Psalms of David." This last work was begun in Jersey, where he completed the first eight Psalms, only the first of which is dated in the manuscript (26 December 1647). In Madrid, he began the ninth Psalm on 13 February 1650 and continued through the sixty-seventh Psalm. The next three were written in Antwerp, the first of which is dated 16 July 1651. The manuscript was later finished during his final exile. Each "reflexion," drawn from the subject matter or particular expressions within the Psalm, is followed by a prayer. The work has no particular literary merit, although it is an interesting index to his state of mind at the time of the successive compositions.

Cromwell's success in subjugating Ireland and the defeat of the Scottish army at Dunbar in September 1650 put an end to any possibility of Scottish aid. With the murder of Antony Ascham, an agent sent by Parliament to the Spanish court, things became increasingly awkward for the two ambassadors. In December 1650, they were asked to leave. Cottington, in his seventies and not well, secured permission to remain in Spain as a private citizen. After nearly sixteen months, Hyde left Spain in March 1651. He went first to Paris to see the queen and then to Antwerp, where he rejoined his wife and family in June 1651.

In December 1651, Hyde returned to Paris at the request of Charles, who had just returned after his escape at Worcester. He had been sworn a councillor to Charles immediately after his father's execution and he now became the king's chief advisor. For the next nine years, Hyde worked to hold the royalist party together. He sought to keep the king firm in his commitment to the Church, to discourage any attempt at securing the support of either Catholics or Presbyterians in exchange for religious concessions, and to prevent any political or personal concessions which might impair the possibility of restoring the monarchy. In the *History* he recorded the political philosophy under which he then acted: "[He] believed that the King had nothing at this time to do but to be quiet, and that all his activity was to consist in carefully avoiding to do any thing that might do him hurt, and to expect some blessed conjuncture from the amity of Christian princes, or some such revolution of affairs in England by their own discontents and divisions amongst themselves, as might make it seasonable for his majesty again to shew himself" (13:140). These years are full of unsuccessful plans; every reasonable suggestion or scheme was explored. This was necessary, if for no other reason, in order to give some semblance of life and hope to the royalist cause. The danger within England itself, though, was that each abortive uprising only provided Cromwell with an additional excuse for strengthening his control and persecuting the king's supporters. For example, with the collapse of a small revolt in Wiltshire in the spring of 1655, Cromwell ordered a decimation tax on all members of the royal party whereby they were to pay a tenth part of their estate to the Commonwealth. In justification of this new policy, Cromwell issued a declaration which was published on 31 October 1655. This was sent to Cologne, where the king ordered Hyde to reply to it. Hyde's answer, published in 1656, is the only known pamphlet which he composed during this eight-year period.[17]

Restoration

The "revolution of affairs" for which Hyde had hoped came with the sudden death of Cromwell on 3 September 1658. Contrary to the expectations of most royalists, this alteration produced no immediate benefit for Charles. Between the time of Cromwell's death and the restoration, Hyde carried on a voluminous correspondence with a broad range of contacts within England. It offers evidence of the bewildering multiplicity of schemes and approaches over which Hyde superintended. It is impossible, of course, to assess Hyde's role in the restoration of the monarchy, for the chain of circumstances within England was quite beyond the control of any single individual. If, however, Hyde was not the architect of the means by which Charles was restored, he was principally responsible for the terms upon which the restoration was effected. It is quite likely, for example, that without Hyde's efforts and guidance, Charles would have been forced to accept the compromises which his father had agreed to at the Treaty on the Isle of Wight, and this included the establishment of Presbyterianism for a three-year period within England. Hyde's basic tactic here were twofold. The first strategy was based upon deferring concessions until they were requested by specific bills of a free parliament. It was this "escape clause" which was so brilliantly embodied in the king's Declaration of Breda, drafted by Hyde. His second was the familiar one of winning men by places. He sought, for example, to secure the support of some moderate Presbyterians by promising them preferments in the Church. Rewards to individual men would prevent the need for any large scale concessions to the whole Presbyterian party.

With the restoration, Hyde's power and control were unrivaled. His position, however, was immediately threatened by the marriage of his daughter Anne to the Duke of York. Prior to the restoration, Anne was a member of the household of the Princess of Orange. During this period, she and the duke agreed to a secret contract of marriage on 24 November 1659. The relationship, forced into the open by Anne's pregnancy, was politically and socially undesirable. Moreover, since Charles himself was unmarried and without legitimate issue, the duke was heir presumptive to the throne. Hyde himself argued against the union, but the duke secretly married Anne on 3 September 1660, in time to legitimatize the child. It was only after a three-month interval of vacilliation, however, that the duke publicly acknowledged the marriage. Charles took this opportunity to display his gratitude to and confidence in Hyde, raising him to the peerage on 3 November 1660 as Baron Hyde of Hindon. On 20 April 1661 he was created Viscount Cornbury and Earl of Clarendon. This elevation was accompanied by a grant from Charles of £20,000.

More serious threats to Clarendon's position soon appeared, and within less than two years, his influence with the king had sharply declined. In the *Continuation* of his autobiography, he attributes this hostility and change of fortune to the "envy" of his opponents. Even during the last years of exile prior to the restoration, there had been a number of attempts to discredit him and to remove him from the king's confidence. In a larger sense, though, Clarendon's fall was inevitable. Ormonde suggested that Clarendon become the prime minister but he refused on the grounds that "England would not bear a favourite, nor any one man, who should out of his ambition engross to himself the disposal of the public affairs" (*Continuation*, 87). Nevertheless, it must have seemed to many that, with or without the title, Clarendon already occupied such a position.

Clarendon played an active role in the restoration settlement. He vigorously supported the Act of Indemnity and Oblivion, signed 29 August 1660, and opposed the efforts of the Commons to enlarge the number of those excepted from pardon. The act provided a land settlement as well in which, "so far ... as there was any principle ... it was to restore crown and church land to its rightful owners; to confirm possession acquired by private contract, and to secure complete restitution for certain favoured persons."[18] The group which was not provided for in any way under the act were those royalists who "voluntarily" sold lands by private contract in order to pay the fines or taxes demanded by the Interregnum government. Such a settlement aroused bitter opposition and was referred to as an act of "indemnity for the King's enemies, and of oblivion for his friends."[19]

Clarendon played an equally prominent role in the settlement of the Church. The Declaration of Breda had offered "a liberty to tender consciences" and a consent "to such an act of parliament as,

upon mature deliberation, shall be offered to us, for the full granting that indulgence."[20] The Presbyterians, remembering that
Charles himself had once subscribed (forcibly) to the Solemn
League and Covenant and feeling that they had contributed significantly to his restoration, expected a genuine modification in the
Church of England. While still in exile, Hyde had directed efforts
toward "winning" the moderate Presbyterian leaders by offering
them bishoprics. He was instrumental as well in filling the vacant
sees and in easing the passage of a bill which restored the bishops to
the House of Lords. Although Clarendon was a firm and enthusias-
tic supporter of the Church of England, it is clear that he hoped that
the moderate Presbyterians would be comprehended within the
Church rather than excluded. The Convention Parliament produced no legislation on the religious settlement. After its adjourn-
ment, the king issued on 25 October 1660 a Declaration of
Ecclesiastical Affairs which was drafted by Clarendon. It referred
the resolution of differences to a national synod and promised a
temporary latitude until then. The synod—the Savoy Conference—failed to produce agreement and the new, predominantly
Anglican Parliament of 1661 quickly produced a series of bills
which ended all hopes of any religious compromise. The most
important of these was the Act of Uniformity, signed on 19 May
1662, which imposed a strict uniformity to the Church of England
as then established by law. In all, it is estimated that nearly 2,000
clergymen were dispossessed in this way.[21] It seems fairly certain
that this repressive measure did not meet with Clarendon's
approval and that he actively sought ways in which to amend or
suspend implementation of the act. At some point in 1663–64,
though, Clarendon's attitude toward toleration appears to have
changed. In the *Continuation* he notes his approval of both the
Conventicle Act of 1664 and the Five Mile Act of 1665 (2:511).
These two statutes form part of what is referred to as the Clarendon Code, although Clarendon himself was not responsible for the
legislation nor is it certain that he fully endorsed it.[22]

Whatever opposition and animosity Clarendon attracted by his
part in the legislative settlement within England, his fall is more
obviously traceable first to a series of events in which as the chief

minister he had a conspicuous role but for which he was not principally responsible, and second, to a pattern of personal behavior which increasingly isolated him from the king. Part of the settlement involved a marriage for Charles. Even prior to the restoration there were plans for a projected alliance with Portugal involving a Catholic Portuguese princess—Catharine of Braganza—and a very large dowry. Clarendon initially urged the king to marry a Protestant but did agree that the proposed terms were such as could not be bettered. The proposal received the approval of the King's council and on 8 May 1661, the decision was announced to Parliament. Prior to the marriage it was rumored that the princess could not have children and when the rumor proved true, Clarendon was accused by many, quite unjustly, of having arranged a barren marriage for the king in order that the succession would go to his daughter's children.[23]

The marriage was strongly supported by France in the hopes of involving English troops in a war against Spain. France sent an agent, Bastide, to confer with Clarendon. Although Clarendon indignantly refused a personal bribe of £10,000 offered by Bastide, acting for Charles he did both solicit and receive considerable sums of money from France, initiating what Lister refers to as "the pensioned dependence of the restored monarch on the King of France."[24] Charles's financial difficulties were also responsible for the sale of Dunkirk. Although Clarendon did not propose the sale, he did argue that if it were sold, France was the only logical buyer and he did conduct the sale negotiations. After the treaty was signed on 27 October 1662 Clarendon was again accused not only of "advising and effecting" the sale but also of sharing in the profit. By 1665, Pepys notes, Clarendon's new house under construction in Piccadilly was by the "common people ... already called Dunkirke-house, from their opinion of his having a good bribe for the selling of that town."[25]

The event which perhaps occasioned the greatest public hostility toward Clarendon was the second Anglo-Dutch War. Clarendon was opposed to it, believing that the king should firmly settle matters at home before engaging in any foreign wars. But such advice was countered by the interests of English merchants and, in particular, the hostile naval actions in Africa and America sanctioned by the Duke of York. War was officially declared on 22 February 1665. As far as the actual conduct of the war, Clarendon seems to have exercised no influence at all. In the *Continuation*, he notes that military strategy was "so much [out] of his sphere, that he never pretended to understand what was fit and reasonable to be done: nor throughout the whole conduct of the war was he ever known to presume to give an advice; but presum[ing] that all whose profession it was advised what was fit, he readily concurred" (2:1026). If Clarendon was not responsible for the military strategy employed in the war, he must, in a larger sense, bear some responsibility for it as an action growing out of a failure of foreign policy. Keith Feiling, for example, has observed that Clarendon was "unfitted to deal with the foreign politics of that age," that "nowhere more than in foreign affairs, for neither in the crucial negotiations in the Spanish peninsula, nor in the inception of the Dutch War and the efforts to close it, did the King's titular chief minister play a chieftain's part."[26]

Looking objectively at Clarendon's seven-year tenure, it is admittedly clear that his interests and accomplishments were in domestic rather than international affairs. Despite the fact that by 1665 Clarendon's authority with both Parliament and the king had sharply eroded, he was still the conspicuous if symbolic head of the government. As the war dragged on, popular opposition to Clarendon mounted. In June 1667, the Dutch fleet entered the Medway, sailing up the river to destroy the English fleet at the naval base of Chatham. The Dutch attack and the astonishing unpreparedness of the King's defenses which it revealed occasioned severe public criticism. Pepys records that on the day of the attack on Chatham, Clarendon's house was beseiged by "some rude people" who "cut down the trees before his house and broke his windows; and a gibbet either set up before or painted upon his gate, and these three words writ: 'Three sights to be seen; Dunkirke, Tangier, and a barren Queene.'"[27] Faced with the threat of invasion by the Dutch, Charles moved quickly to raise an army, but he needed money to pay it. Parliament, the only source of supply, was prorogued until October. Arguing that Parliament could not legally be summoned into session before October, Clarendon advised the king either to dissolve this Parliament and immediately issue writs for a new one or to raise money through prerogative measures. In the course of debate, Clarendon apparently spoke of Parliament as "four hundred men...only of use to raise...money, but...not fit to meddle with state affairs."[28] This remark and his suggestion that money be raised by prerogative measures were later to be used in his attempted impeachment. Clarendon's advice was ignored and Parliament assembled on 25 July 1667. In the interval peace had been concluded at Breda on 21 July and Charles was forced to prorogue the session on 29 July. The resentment of the House of Commons, carefully manipulated by his enemies, and the rising indignation of the populace, centered on Clarendon; he was to be the scapegoat.

Impeachment and Exile

Unquestionably Clarendon was not guilty of much of what he was accused of, but his position and behavior made him the inevitable and vulnerable target for criticism. Out of the vast supply for the war granted by Parliament, an incredible sum, perhaps as high as £2,390,000, had been siphoned off for the private use of the court.[29] There is no evidence to suggest that Clarendon shared in this spoil or that he was guilty, in seventeenth-century terms, of the corruption and bribery which formed the basis of nine of the seventeen charges in his impeachment. But the great mansion he was building, under construction throughout the war years, seemed to the people a conspicuous symbol of the corruption and mismanagement of Charles's government.

Popular antagonism alone toward Clarendon could not, of course, have caused his fall. But Clarendon had powerful enemies in both Parliament and the Court. His concept of proper governmental administration centered around a strong privy council, composed of a relatively few powerful heads of the various departments of state. Such a council, in Clarendon's view, would serve to "restrain the encroachments of parliament, while respecting its privileges, and...to check the undue influence of unofficial favourites."

Under this system, "the legislative functions were to be committed to the king in parliament, while the whole superintendence of the executive was to be entrusted to the king in council."[30] Clarendon resisted all attempts at administrative reform, many of which were desperately needed, and actively opposed attempts by the Commons to extend their authority. These two factors figured prominently in his downfall, despite the fact that Clarendon himself attributed his destruction almost exclusively to personal animosities. There were, of course, within Parliament and the court, many eager place-seekers who were anxious to see him removed. Moreover, his penchant for formality, his physical size, his lameness (from gout), his pompous and morally self-righteous bearing, and his frequently magisterial tone to Charles made him an object of ridicule and no doubt contributed significantly to Charles's growing dissatisfaction with him. Probably the most powerful influence working against him, though, was Lady Castlemaine, Charles's reigning mistress, of whom Clarendon had always disapproved.

Convinced by the arguments of Clarendon's enemies, Charles felt that he must remove the chancellor before Parliament reassembled in October. Charles wrote to Ormonde: "The truth is, his behaviour and humour was grown so unsupportable to myself, and to all the world else, that I could not longer endure it, and it was impossible for me to live with it, and do those things with the Parliament that must be done, or the Government will be lost."[31] With the assistance of the Duke of York, Charles first tried to persuade Clarendon to resign. Confident in his innocence and his ability to defend himself, Clarendon was unwilling to resign voluntarily. Finally, on 30 August 1667, Charles was forced to send secretary Morrice with a royal warrant for him to deliver the seals of his office. Clarendon did so, planning then to retire quietly into the country.

It soon became apparent, however, that his enemies wanted more than just his removal from office. Shortly after Parliament opened on 10 October 1667, it appointed a committee to draw up charges of high treason against Clarendon. On 6 November the committee made its report, which contained seventeen charges. Only one charge—betraying the king's secrets to an enemy—

constituted treason and all were extremely tenuous, if not completely false, and probably unprovable anyway. On 12 November the impeachment was carried to the Lords with the request that Clarendon be placed in custody until the charge could be proved. The Lords refused to commit because no exact charge had been made. While the Houses were thus deadlocked, Charles made it quite clear that he wanted Clarendon to leave the country. Confident that he could not be found guilty, Clarendon delayed. Finally, yielding to the persuasion of the Duke of York and the Bishop of Hereford, and afraid that Charles might well dissolve Parliament and allow him to be tried by a court of selected peers, Clarendon left England on 29 November 1667, arriving in Calais three days later. He left behind a written statement of vindication addressed to the Lords.[32] With Clarendon gone, however, his guilt was assumed by many. The two Houses concurred in a bill of banishment, signed by the king, which made it high treason for him to return to England after a set date and made his pardon impossible without Parliament's consent.[33]

For the first six months of his exile, he had little rest, moving from Calais to Rouen, back to Calais, on to the baths at Bourbon and then to Avignon. It was not until July 1668, when Clarendon settled in Montpellier, that he was able to attain a degree of peace. In his imposed leisure, he turned immediately to writing. His first thought was of a formal, written vindication of himself from the charges of treason. He began this work, "A Discourse, by Way of Vindication of my self from the Charge of High-Treason...," on 24 July 1668. He realized that such a work could not be published in England, but he wrote it for "the information of his children and other friends, to vindicate himself from those aspersions and reproaches which the malice of his enemies had cast upon him in the parliament" (*Continuation*, 2:1243). At the same time he started his autobiography, the first page dated 23 July 1668. By 1 August 1670 Clarendon had completed the last of the seven parts of the original *Life*.

During this period he also finished his shorter pieces, collected as "Reflections upon several Christian Duties, Divine and Moral, By way of Essays" and first published in *A Collection of several*

Tracts of ... Edward, earl of Clarendon in 1727, and his "Contemplations and Reflexions upon the Psalms of David" (q.v.). His "reflexions" on the first 70 Psalms had been written prior to this final exile. While in Montpellier he completed the rest, beginning on 13 December 1668 and ending on 27 February 1670. He was also at work on his answer to Hobbes's *Leviathan,* published in 1676 as *A Brief View and Survey of the Dangerous and pernicious Errors to Church and State, in Mr. Hobbes's Book, Entitled Leviathan.* In the text of this book he notes that he finished the manuscript in April 1670, although some changes in at least the form of the reply were probably made in 1673. Under the act of banishment, it was a treasonable act to correspond with him; consequently, there is almost no correspondence which dates from the final exile. The few surviving exceptions are some personal letters, generally to his sons, and several public appeals addressed to the royal family. He wrote, for example, to both the Duke and Duchess of York in 1670 when he heard that his daughter, the duchess, had converted to Catholicism (*Clarendon State Papers,* 3:supplement, xxxvii-xxxviii;xxxviii-xl).[34]

By June 1671, he had moved from Montpellier to Moulins, apparently in order to make it easier for his son Laurence to visit him. At the request of his father, Laurence brought with him a number of manuscripts and papers, including the manuscript of the original version of the *History* which Clarendon had begun in Jersey in 1646. Clarendon set to work immediately combining this manuscript with the newly finished autobiography. By 8 June 1672, the composite was probably finished, for on that day he began work on the *Continuation* of his autobiography. This work begins with the restoration, covers the years of Clarendon's administration, and ends with his present exile. Just as Clarendon had exposed the "dangerous and pernicious" errors in the political theory set forth in *Leviathan,* so now he turned to expose the threats which Catholicism posed to the civil government in two additional commentaries. The first was published in 1674 as *Animadversions upon a Book, Intituled Fanaticism Fanatically Imputed to the Catholick Church, by Dr. Stillingfleet, and the Imputation Refuted and Retorted by S. C.* As its title indicates, it is part of a chain of six published exchanges between Edward Stillingfleet, a minor Anglican divine, and Serenus Cressy (Hugh Paulinus Cressy), a converted Catholic. Clarendon's second work, begun during his embassy in Spain, is a much more ambitious survey of the history of the papacy. It is dated at the end of the manuscript from Moulins, 12 February 1674. It was not published until 1811 as *Religion and Policy*.

At some point between April and July 1674, Clarendon moved from Moulins to Rouen perhaps with the hope that he might be able to return home. From Rouen in mid-August he wrote to Charles, the queen, and the Duke of York asking for permission to return. To Charles he wrote:

It is now full seven years since I have been deprived of your Majesty's favour, with some circumstances of mortification which have never been exercised towards any other man, and therefore I may hope from your good nature and justice, that a severity which you have never practised upon any other man for half the time, may be diminished in some degree towards me... that I may return to beg my bread in England, and to die amongst my own children. (*Clarendon State Papers*, 3:supplement, xliv)

The request was not granted and Clarendon died in Rouen on 9 December 1674. His body was returned to England where, on 4 January 1675, he was buried in Westminster Abbey.

Chapter Two
The *History of the Rebellion:*
Its Composition

Clarendon's *History of the Rebellion* is the product of three distinct periods of composition spanning twenty-five years. He began work on it immediately after fleeing from England with the Prince of Wales in 1646, but was forced to stop two years later when he was summoned to France to rejoin him. Clarendon did not resume work until after his banishment from England in 1668, at which point he began his "Life." Then in 1670 he took the original "History" and the completed "Life" and spliced them together, adding some new material, to make the final *History of the Rebellion.* The final *History* thus resulted from fusing together two separate works which had distinctly different intentions and methods. Questions of structure, selectivity, and purpose in the final *History* are, correspondingly, difficult to answer—certainly more difficult than they would be if the *History* had been the product of a single (no matter how extended) period of composition governed by a sustained, consistent purpose. This chapter examines first, Hyde's original "History," written from 1646–48; second, his "Life" written in 1668–71; and finally, the *History* as it emerged in 1671–72.

The Original "History of the Rebellion"

Until Edward Hyde fled from England with the Prince of Wales in March 1646, he had written little more than royalist pamphlets and speeches. After his flight he continued his efforts for the royalist cause by beginning the original version of the "History" almost immediately after he arrived on the Scilly Islands—the first page of the manuscript dated "Silly, March 18, 1645[6]."[1] He explained his desire to begin his work so quickly in a letter to Secretary Nicholas: "As soon as I found myself alone, I thought the best way to provide myself for new business against the time I should be called to it ... was to look over the faults of the old; and so I resolved ... to write a history of these evil times" (*Clarendon State Papers*, 2:288). Hyde's original intention was to compile, in the form of an historical narrative, an instructive guide to past mistakes, and by implication, to future political conduct. His history, by isolating those errors which led to the "rebellion," would be a valuable contribution to practical politics.

Judging from the letters which date from this first period of composition, it seems that Hyde never intended for his "History" to be published, at least in its original form: "I write with all fidelity and freedom of all I know, of persons and things, and the oversights and omissions on both sides" (*Clarendon State Papers*, 2:289). In this sense, the original "History" was, as H. R. Trevor-Roper has observed, "a state paper by a faithful servant who took his duties seriously."[2]

The original "History" consisted of seven books, one of which was only a sketchy outline. Hyde began with the death of King James in 1625, and by the time that he was forced to stop writing, he had brought his narrative to the start of the campaign of 1644. The first book of the "History"—what Hyde called his "prolegomenon"—deals with the "state of affairs and conditions" from the death of King James through the beginning of the first session of the Long Parliament. The emphasis is suggested by the choice of the word "prolegomenon," for this book is a prelude to or preparation for the chain of events which began with the summoning of the Long Parliament. Book I is largely a narrative catalogue of royalist errors. It is not designed as a documentary history of the origins of the rebellion, but rather as a background to explain how and why the royalist position had so completely deteriorated by the opening of the Long Parliament. For Hyde, the rebellion occurred not because of irresistible social, or economic, or religious issues, but because of the failures, mistakes, and intentional actions of a small group of men responsible for governing the kingdom. The royalist errors, for Hyde, came in two areas.

The first type of error occurred in the clumsy statecraft of Charles and his advisors in dissolving three successive parliaments.

As one would expect from a royal servant, Hyde places the responsibility not upon Charles himself, but upon his advisors. The real danger in the dissolutions lay in the subsequent violation of the constitutional rights of the people. Pressed as he was by financial need, and faced with the fact that successive parliaments, in part because of their rapid dissolution, had failed to grant adequate subsidies, Charles was forced to use "supplemental acts of state" to gather the monies which had not been granted by law. When the legality of those impositions was challenged and the king's right upheld by the judges, it only served to undermine the people's confidence in and respect for the law.

The second area in which the king and his advisors made serious errors was in the handling of the two Scottish wars. Again the fault lay with the incompetent, inadequate, and often pernicious advice Charles received from his advisors. Pitted against what seemed to Hyde an incredible array of royalist blunders were the shrewd propagandistic and political tactics of the Scots. In order to deal with the Scottish settlement, Charles was forced to call another parliament—the Long Parliament.

In Book II Hyde provides a detailed analysis of the first session of the Long Parliament, which met from 3 November 1640 through 20 October 1641. Book I had concentrated on royalist blunders; Book II seeks to document the strategies by which a small group of men in both houses managed to deprive the king of a parliamentary base of support, to deprive him of adequate and honest advice, and to infringe upon and curtail royal rights and perogatives. Hyde's sympathies for the king's position are clearly obvious, so much so, in fact, that Sir Charles Firth has observed that "there is no part of the original 'History' which demands more careful scrutiny, none in which his partisanship is more obvious and his representation of facts more one-sided."[3]

Hyde cites at length a number of ways in which the parliamentary minority gained control of the House of Commons: excluding or frightening away those members with strong royalist sympathies, impeaching Strafford and Laud, and encouraging seditious preaching and printing. Deprived of sound advice, Charles was forced to give his approval to a series of laws which restricted royal prerogative. At the end of Book II, Hyde summarizes each of those "concessions," stressing the gradual shift of power from the crown to Parliament. Hyde's royalist sympathies are nowhere more evident than at the end of this book where he comments on this series of laws to which Charles agreed: "[They] will be hereafter acknowledged by an incorrupted posterity to be everlasting monuments of a princely and fatherly affection to his people, and such an obligation of repose and trust from the King in the hearts of his subjects that no expressions of piety, duty, and confidence, from them, could have been more than a sufficient return on their parts" (3:271).

Book III of the original "History" (now Book IV) begins with the king's arrival in York on his way to Scotland to conclude officially the second Scots war in August 1641, and ends, symmetrically, with the king's arrival in York in March 1642, prior to the outbreak of the first civil war. Within these limits, the book continues the detailed narrative of the struggle for power between the king and the Long Parliament as controlled by what Hyde calls the "ministers of confusion." Hyde's extensive analysis of the Long Parliament is, in part, a reflection of his own increasing involvement in that struggle as a member of Parliament.

What Hyde criticizes is Parliament's growing departures from a constitutional base. These "ministers of confusion" were overturning the old order, extending their authority far beyond any constitutionally justifiable position, and infringing upon royal right and prerogative. Hyde was an ardent supporter of royal power, provided it was exercised within proper constitutional channels. Charles had admittedly violated those limits, but so had Parliament. A proper balance, and for Hyde it was a conservative balance in favor of the monarch, must be maintained.

Book IV, now Book V of the final *History*, begins with the arrival of the king in York on 19 March 1642 and ends with the king erecting his standard at Nottingham on 22 August 1642. The book is one of the longest in the original (and the final) "History" and is made so in large part by Hyde's inclusion of large numbers of papers, petitions, declarations, and manifestos issued by the king and by Parliament. Some of these documents are printed in their entirety; others are summarized. The inclusion of so many documents disrupts the narrative, and Hyde was well aware of this. One can speculate on several reasons why Hyde chose to include the documents nonetheless. Certainly, as Firth has pointed out, there was a sense of self-justification and pride involved.[4] The declarations and the policy they enunciated were of Hyde's making. Moreover, they, more than anything else, were an adequate representation of the events of the period—one, as Hyde said, "wholly spent in talk." The real significance of this interval of time lay in the creation and articulation of a defensible, coherent policy for the king. This was done through the documents prepared by Hyde and issued under the king's name. To include them in the "History" is to recreate, for the reader at least, a rhetorical credibility for the king's positions and actions.

The emphasis of Book IV of the original "History" shifts from the activities in Parliament toward those of the king and his handful of loyal supporters. This is occasioned by the fact that in May 1642 Hyde left London to join Charles; it is natural then that the focus of the narrative should shift as well. Hyde is increasingly concerned not merely with justifying the king's theoretical or political position (a defense resting largely upon the included documents) but also with justifying the king's course of action—or the lack of it—during those early months.

The original Book V of the "History" was never finished. It was to "contain a discourse of the just Regal power of the Kings of England, and of his negative voice, of the Militia, and of the Great Seal, by the laws of the Kingdom, of the original, at least of the antiquity and constitution of Parliaments, of their jurisdiction and privileges, of the power of the House of Peers by the law, and of the natural limits and extent of the Commons" (*Clarendon State Papers*, 2:334). In the original manuscript, Hyde had skipped eighty pages to allow for its inclusion. An outline, noted by Macray (6:note 1), is all that survives. Presumably Hyde never finished the projected book because the necessary materials never arrived in Jersey.[5] Even though there are scattered observations on each of the topics in these early books of the "History," it is unfortunate that Hyde did not finish the book at that time. Had he done so, it would have offered important documentation of his political theory in the

1640s. Further, its projection is at least additional confirmation of the pragmatic nature of the original "History." Much of the material is covered, though, in an anonymous book published in 1645 and now attributed to Hyde.[6] The theoretical and digressive nature of this projected book might well have been an argument against its completion. When Hyde returned to work on the *History* in the 1670s, he saw it no longer as a practical guide to politics, but as an historical work. As a result, such a digression might well have seemed out of place.

Books VI and VII of the original "History" are predominantly narratives of military actions. Hyde's intention was to devote a book to each year of the war, the year ending in the old style of dating in March rather than in December. Thus, Book VI covers the period from the king's erecting his standard at Nottingham, 22 August 1642, through the events of late March and early April 1643; Book VII, the period from the peace negotiations in Oxford, February-April 1643, through the siege of Newark and its relief by Prince Rupert on 22 March 1644. As a record of the military aspects of these years, the "History" is very spotty. Although Hyde is generally reliable about what he includes, he is by no means thorough in his coverage of the war. Throughout the first war years—from October 1642 through March 1645—Hyde stayed in Oxford. To make up for this, he sought the assistance of others. Hyde's coverage depends upon his success in securing such additional information; some parts of the war are treated in great detail; others are barely mentioned or are omitted completely.

The value of the *History* does not rest on its factual accuracy and thoroughness. Had Hyde been able to secure the information he desired, the final *History* would have been several times as long as it is now. But Hyde realized the simple impossibility of such a task and, at a number of points in the text, indicated the limits he had imposed on his coverage. He avoids any detailed treatment of events in either Scotland or Ireland; he exercises considerable selectiveness in treating the military campaigns. The selectivity is not always necessitated by the lack for information, for Hyde is always more interested in the motivations and actions of individual men than he is in the specific details of battle. Time and again Hyde turns away from a mere recitation of events toward an analysis of their context and significance. He is valuable for his account of the state of the king's party in Oxford during the early war years; he is always insightful about the clashes of personality which so often hampered the effective conduct of the war, both in terms of particular military actions and in terms of the longer range policy decisions.

Similarly, he is much more interested in the attempts at negotiating a peace, no matter how unsuccessful they were, than he is in military maneuvers. This can be explained in part by the fact that Hyde played an important part in such attempts, if not directly as a negotiator such as at Uxbridge, then indirectly as the "author" of Charles's printed positions. At each juncture, he inserts the text of the relevant documents. His concern is to show that, from his point of view, he and the king did everything that could be reasonably expected toward ending the war.

Hyde's "History" does have other limitations. In places, such as in the vindication of Charles's conduct toward the Irish rebels, Hyde unwittingly reveals his ignorance of some of the king's private strategies. And throughout, although Hyde never hesitates to criticize the inadequacies and mistakes made by individual members of the king's party, he rarely offers any criticism of the whole royalist position. For Hyde, the war was waged by a "violent party" who, once a minority, became a majority in Parliament because of the withdrawal and flight of so many of its original members. All efforts toward peace, Hyde maintains, were thwarted by the willful actions of that faction.

Hyde never got much further in his narrative. Book VII is dated at the end of the manuscript "Castle Elizabeth, 8. of March. 1647[8]." Hyde left Jersey on 26 June 1648 to join the queen and the Prince of Wales in France. In the three months he had just barely begun what would be Book VIII. He left two other pieces of manuscript. One, endorsed in his hand "Concerning the westerne businesse," was an account of the campaign in the West in 1645–46.[7] Hyde apparently intended to use this when his narrative reached 1645. It was later incorporated into the final *History* in Books IX and X. A second much shorter fragment—dealing with the prince's Council and the Duke of Hamilton—was also later used in the *History*.[8] This then was the state of the original "History"—six complete books and parts of three more—when Hyde was forced to stop writing and leave Jersey to join the Prince of Wales in France. Hyde never again worked on the manuscript until 1671, when he used it in completing his *History of the Rebellion*.

The "Life"

After his banishment from England in November 1667, Clarendon returned to writing. Once he had settled in Montpellier in July 1668, he immediately began his "Vindication" from the specific charges of treason. At the same time, he set to work on his "Life," the first page dated 23 July 1668. During his three-year stay in Montpellier (July 1668 to June 1671), he worked on the manuscript.

The "Life" begins with an account of his family and ends with the restoration of Charles II in 1660, but it is hardly autobiographical in the sense that we might expect. Most of the "Life" consists of a narrative of public events from the 1630s to 1660. The Clarendon we read about is the public, not the private, man. Several reasons can be suggested for this emphasis: first, Clarendon was not writing an autobiography but a memoir. The difference between the two is indicated by Roy Pascal: "In the autobiography proper, attention is focused on the self, in the memoir or reminiscence on others."[9] Second, what was important to Clarendon was his career, both as a member of Parliament and as a royal servant under two kings. The selectivity of the "Life" clearly reveals this bias: Clarendon records his birth and childhood in one paragraph, his education at Oxford in another, and his role in the first session of the Long Parliament in over fifty pages. Such an example suggests a third reason why Clarendon, beginning to write in 1668 after his banishment and public disgrace, would choose to write about his role in the "rebellion" and restoration. Faced with great hostility and with a king who had willingly, even anxiously, sacrificed him, Clarendon undertook, first, a vindication of himself from the specific charges of treason, and then, second, a full-scale account of his life as a royal servant. The "Life" as Clarendon originally conceived of it was a public document.

The original "Life" is an enormously long work—614 folio manuscript pages—in seven parts.[10] The "Life" in its original form as described in this section exists only in manuscript. When Clarendon began compiling the final version of the *History of the Rebellion*, he used nearly all of the manuscript "Life." What was left, or nearly all of what was left, was finally published separately as the *Life of Edward Hyde, Earl of Clarendon*. Because it is composed of pieces which were not used in the *History*, the published *Life* bears little resemblance to the original "Life" and, moreover, has no integrity as a complete work.

Even though the "Life" survives only as it appears in either the *History* or the *Life*, it still has considerable importance. The value of the *History*, for example, as a source of factual information about the events of the period, depends upon whether the particular section in question came from the original "History" or from the "Life." Both works cover the same period of time, but their accuracy differs considerably. For all of the problems that Hyde had in obtaining information for the "History," he was still closer in time to the events of the 1640s and had access to many documents, letters, and contributions. In the period in which he worked on the "Life" he had neither advantage. The "Life" was written completely from memory and Clarendon's memory of events was not always accurate or precise. This is not to slight the value of the "Life." It adds much to the original narrative, especially in its shrewder and more critical assessment of events and personalities.

Part I of the "Life" covers essentially the same period of time which is covered in the first three books of the final *History*. Clarendon begins with an account of his family and closes with the end of the first session of the Long Parliament in the fall of 1641. From the very outset of the "Life," there is a tension between the two voices: the autobiographer who narrates events that touched his life and the historian who, more impartially, records the signifi-

cant whether it is related directly to his life or not. Clarendon, for
example, begins with a sketchy account of his life to the point when
he entered Middle Temple to study law. It was at the same time that
the Duke of Buckingham was assassinated. Clarendon immediately
begins a very long digression on the duke's life and his rise to
power, never once attempting to establish any relationship
between these events and those of his own life. In the early parts of
the "Life" many of the digressions, like this one, introduce character sketches—groups of verbal portraits of those in power. Indeed,
one of the principal differences between the "History" and the
"Life" is the presence of these sketches. In Part I Clarendon
sketches, in addition to the Duke of Buckingham, the characters of
the chief ministers under Charles I in 1628, his own circle of
friends, and the "great contrivers" who guided the Parliamentary
opposition to Charles I.

Not all of the digressions from the autobiographical account are
concerned with characters. A second very long digression in Part I
is a detailed analysis of the origins and conduct of the first Scots
war. The events and mistakes are catalogued at great length.
Another principal difference between the "History" and the "Life"
is that in the latter Clarendon's analyses of events and men are
more penetrating and his criticisms considerably sharper.

Despite the digressions, though, the focus of the early parts of
the "Life" is on Mr. Hyde's (as he refers to himself) role in
Parliament, especially in the first session of the Long Parliament.
His claims for his own importance in that session must be carefully
compared with contemporary evidence. B. H. G. Wormald has
examined Clarendon's role in the first session in some detail and
his findings reveal the extent to which Clarendon, writing in 1668
of events which took place twenty-five years earlier, misrepresents
his own part and position in that session.[11] It is clear, for example,
that Mr. Hyde was not quite the champion of the Church that
Clarendon represents him to be. We expect selectivity and we
expect that in his "Life" Clarendon would emphasize those actions
or incidents which most favorably represent his role. Sometimes,
however, the omissions are equally interesting. In the original

"History," for instance, there is a long account of the trial of Strafford and the passage of the bill of attainder. The incident, however, is completely ignored in the "Life." Despite his recognition of Strafford's efficiency, Hyde had in 1641 actively supported that impeachment and had, almost certainly, voted for the bill of attainder. Whether or not Clarendon in 1669 regretted his position of 1641, the whole incident would now have had a painful significance to the exiled Clarendon that Mr. Hyde could never have anticipated. Strafford, ruthless and vindictive as he was, remained a faithful servant of the king who was sacrificed because of the clamors of Parliament and the people. Clarendon had not in 1668 forfeited his life, but he was just as surely sacrificed by a king as Strafford had been.

Part II of the "Life" covers the events contained within Books IV through VI of the final *History*. It begins with the king's trip into Scotland in autumn 1641 and ends with the events of late March and early April 1643. It was during this period that Hyde's affiliation with Charles became official and Clarendon relates his new role at some length. The magisterial, and self-rightous, tone that characterizes the narrator of the "Life" is never clearer than in the sketch that he offers of himself:

He had a very particular devotion and passion for the person of the king; and did believe him the most, and the best Christian in the world. He had a most zealous esteem and reverence for the constitution of the government; and believed it so equally poised, that if the least branch of the prerogative was torn off, or parted with, the subject suffered by it, and that his right was impaired; and he was as much troubled when the crown exceeded its just limits, and thought its prerogative hurt by it: and therefore not only never consented to any diminution of the king's authority, but always wished that the king would not consent to it... He had taken more pains than such men use to do, in the examination of religion... and... he did really believe the church of England the most exactly formed and framed for the encouragement and advancement of learning and piety, and for the preservation of peace, of any church in the world... that the diminishing the lustre it had, and had always had in the government, by removing the bishops out of the house of peers, was a violation of justice; the removing a landmark, and the shaking the very foundation of government; and therefore he always opposed, upon the impulsion of conscience, all mutations in the church. (*Life*, 2:14-15)

One early critic, objecting to such a tone, noted that "speaking often of himself, and of Affairs on which he had given Advice, or wherein he had employed, he always represents himself, (perhaps thro' Inadvertency,) extreamly Sage, Reserv'd, and Circumspect; and often gives ill Ideas of the King's other Servants, either as to their Understanding or Management."[12] In defense of Clarendon, it is both fair and accurate to say that had the king been willing to adhere to Hyde's policies, the war might never had occurred.

As Clarendon draws closer to the war years, he is increasingly selective in his detail. Generally he avoids any summary of incidents of which he had no direct knowledge. He omits as well the whole account of the "paper skirmishes" between Parliament and himself, all of which was covered at great length in the original "History." One would expect just the opposite in a memoir. But it is possible that the omission might have been occasioned by the knowledge that such things had already been treated in the "History." It is also true that without documentary evidence at hand, any attempt to reconstruct a paper propaganda war waged twenty-five years earlier would have been impossible.

Part III of the "Life," used in Books VII and VIII of the *History*, covers the period from the peace negotiations at Oxford in March 1644 to the negotiations at Uxbridge one year later. Clarendon had played an important role in both, and here too he offers the reader an "inside" view. Of Oxford, he writes: "Only what passed in secret, and was never communicated, nor can otherwise be known, since at this time no man else is living who was privy to that negociation but [himself] will have a proper place in this discourse" (*Life*, 3:4). Of Uxbridge, he notes: "Only such particulars as fell out in that time and were never communicated, and many of them known to very few, shall be shortly mentioned" (8:220). Clarendon can be detailed (and self-justifying) when he played a crucial role in particular events such as these.

By this point in the "Life," however, Clarendon is beginning to show more and more interest in chronicling significant public events. He is increasingly torn between the two alternatives. He begins to list events in topic form and then dismiss them at the end of a sentence or paragraph with a statement such as "all [are] fitter subjects for the history of that time than for this narration" (7:note to 38). Part IV of the "Life" clearly exhibits this change. All that exists are several pages of notes setting down the outline for the book in topic form. It was to cover events in the West from the prince's departure from Oxford in March 1645 to his departure from Jersey in July 1646. Clarendon did not bother to finish this part because he had already written a narrative account of the period during his first exile in Jersey in 1648 ("Concerning the westerne businesse"). All that was necessary was to secure the original manuscript and rework it. This plan was noted in the surviving outline (*Life*, 4:1–4). This is the first point at which Clarendon notes the existence of a prior document and it signals a change in his plan.

Part V of the "Life" covers the period now treated from Book X to the second third of Book XII of the *History*. Because of the hiatus in Part IV, the narrative begins with the treatment of the king after he joined the Scots in May 1646 and ends prior to Clarendon's first audience with the King of Spain in December 1649. During that period Hyde had spent two years alone on Jersey working on his "History." Removed as he was from the action in England or in France, Clarendon lacked adequate knowledge of the period. The sections which deal with events prior to his rejoining the Prince of Wales in France in September 1648 lack substance, proportion, and coherence. With his return to public life late in 1648, Clarendon's narrative becomes fuller and more valuable, although again its scope is largely restricted to incidents in which he played some part or of which he had some specific information. Clarendon was increasingly aware of the inadequacies of his narrative. At the end of this part of the "Life" he again makes reference to his earlier work, adding a note to the final page of the manuscript indicating that whenever he secured his papers, he intended to make additions and changes (12:note to 99).

Part VI of the "Life," now the latter third of Book XII through Book XIV of the *History*, covers a six-year period from the audience with the King of Spain (1649) through Hyde's pamphlet answer (1654) to Cromwell's decimation tax on the royalists. The account principally records Charles II's shifting fortunes, the difficulties among the exiled court, and Cromwell's attempts to stabilize the government at home. Although Clarendon touches upon some of his personal difficulties, especially with the Queen Mother, he includes only one family incident, the inclusion of which prompts an apology: "Not pertinent to the public history of that time, but necessary to be inserted in the particular relation of the chancellor's life; which had afterwards an influence upon his fortune, and a very great one upon the peace and quiet of his mind, and of his family" (*Life*, 6:38). The incident was the preferment of his daughter Anne in the household of the Princess of Orange. Anne was later to marry the Duke of York.

All of Part VII of the "Life" is contained in Books XV and XVI of the *History*. It begins with an assessment of the conditions within the three kingdoms in 1655 and ends with the restoration of Charles II in 1660. The narrative focuses almost exclusively on public events rather than on private incidents in Clarendon's own life. When he does make a reference to his accepting the position of Lord High Chancellor of England in January 1658, he again apologizes: "Which particular is only fit to be mentioned because many great affairs and some alterations accompanied, though not attended upon, it" (15:83).

By the point at which Clarendon reached Part IV of his "Life" (in late 1669), he seems to have changed his mind about the nature of the work he was writing. As we saw earlier in this section, there was always a tension between Clarendon the autobiographer and Clarendon the historian of the age. The early parts of the "Life" are more autobiography than history. When Clarendon digresses into the events of the age he often apologizes for including matter "foreign to the proper subject of this discourse" (2:65). The further that he wrote into the "Life," however, the more the balance changed. There is increasingly less reference to his part in the public affairs, despite the fact that his power and position significantly increase. By the late 1650s Clarendon is a more important figure in the exiled government of Charles II than he ever was under Charles I. But by the final parts of the "Life" he has disappeared: where before Clarendon apologizes for digressions into public affairs, he now apologizes for even mentioning a personal incident. What happened as he wrote further into the "Life" is that Clarendon was gradually drawn away from autobiography into the larger perspective of writing history. There is, unfortunately, no surviving external evidence which would indicate at what point Clarendon decided to sacrifice his "Life" for the *History*. The accepted thesis, also without external evidence, is that Clarendon had not thought of his *History* until after Laurence brought the original manuscript to him in June 1671. It seems more likely, however, that at some undatable point between 1668 and 1670 Clarendon began to plan to integrate the two works. The latter parts of the "Life" were, for example, transferred in toto into the *History*. There was no need for changes because by the time he was working on Part VII of the "Life" Clarendon had abandoned his autobiography for history. It only remained for him to combine the two manuscripts into the final *History of the Rebellion*.

The *History of the Rebellion*

The further that Clarendon wrote in the "History" and in the "Life," the more he departed from what were his original intentions in each case. The original "History" was to have been a guide to statecraft; it began with an assessment of the errors made and of the positions which should have prevailed. But by the late books, this aspect changed. The "History" became, more simply, a record of the events of the "rebellion." The "Life" began with recognizably autobiographical detail but later these were subsumed into a record of the age. Both works move toward the direction taken by the final *History of the Rebellion*.

The final part of the "Life"—the account of the restoration of Charles II—had been finished by 1 August 1670. In early June 1671 Clarendon moved from Montpellier to Moulins to meet his son Laurence. He had directed Laurence to bring from England his papers, among which was the manuscript of the original "History" written during his first exile in 1646 to 1648. Clarendon had apparently been planning to integrate the "History" and the "Life" for some time. Firth suggests that the whole process of dovetailing the two earlier works together and the writing of a small additional amount of text was completed within a year—beginning immediately after the visit of his son in June 1671 and ending 8 June 1672, the day on which Clarendon began the "Continuation" of his "Life."[13]

Presumably several factors lay behind Clarendon's decision to finish his "History," not the least of which was probably his desire to leave his mark on the tradition of English historical writing. Another more expedient reason is support of Clarendon's appeal to Charles II to repeal the banishment and allow him to return home to die. Correspondingly, Clarendon represents his efforts on the *History* and on his reply to Hobbes's *Leviathan* as acts of service to both kings. The expediency of such a tactic is even more obvious in Clarendon's letter to Charles II, 11 June [1672]. After thanking him for allowing his son to visit him in France and asking "leave to cast myself at your feet," Clarendon continues:

My banishment hath hitherto been the more supportable to me, in that I think I have performed a work, under this mortification, which I began with the approbation and encouragement of your blessed Father, and when I had the honour to be near your Majesty, and which, if I do not overmuch flatter myself, may be for the honour of both your Majesties. *(Clarendon State Papers,* 3:supplement x1)

Charles, of course, never relented and Clarendon died in exile.

The process of compiling the final *History* came in two stages. For Books I through VII, Clarendon simply spliced together relevant and related sections of the two manuscripts, occasionally making minor changes and adding transitional passages. The original "History" stopped, however, with the end of what is now Book VII. For Books VIII through XVI Clarendon had only the material contained in the "Life." For these final books then he was forced to write additional material to fill out the narrative. These two stages offer a convenient way of looking at the process by which the final *History* emerged.

In the first seven books of the *History*, three-fourths of the text comes from the original "History" and one-fourth from the "Life." In several places Clarendon transferred large blocks from the "Life" into the "History." In Book I, for example, he inserted the long digression about the Duke of Buckingham, the character sketches of the ministers under Charles I in 1628, and the account of the origin and nature of the ecclesiastical dispute which led to the first Scottish war. In other places, such as in Book IV, Clarendon switches back and forth between the two manuscripts, sometimes transferring as little as a paragraph or a sentence. The bulk of the material taken from the "Life" comes, however, in the opening books. By the time the narrative reaches the war years (Books V through VII), the final text is overwhelmingly taken from the original "History."

The material transferred from the "Life" consists predominantly of character sketches of influential men, analyses of the roles played by individuals or by Mr. Hyde himself in particular actions, anecdotal material, and some passages of generalized assessment of the "state and temper" of the time. The addition of material which is primarily concerned with individuals—their characters, motivations, and actions—greatly strengthens the emphasis upon the importance of personal causes in the final *History*. Moreover, Clarendon's criticisms of individuals in the "Life" were considerably sharper than those in the first "History." Adding the material from the "Life" does change the original tone of these books. The analysis of the roles individuals played seems now shrewder, more specific.

In some instances Clarendon is fairly careful to provide an adequate rationale for the fusion. He transferred into the "History" in the first seven books sixty-four character sketches. For the large groups of these—the ministers in 1628 (Book I), the leaders of the Parliamentary opposition (Book III), the king's Privy Councillors (Book VI)—he wrote transition passages such as the one in Book I. Where he can supplement the treatment in the original "History" he does so, such as in Book III where he used all of the account of the

Long Parliament written for the "Life" except two passages, one of which extolled his own efforts (now *Life*, 1:85-88) and another which recorded three conversations (now *Life*, 1:89-95). When he reaches the war years, he adds to the narrative sections from the "Life" which are short, personal, and largely anecdotal in nature.

As such additions suggest, in most cases the material taken from the "Life" supplements that in the "History." Where Clarendon had written two accounts of the same action he was faced with a choice, and it is not possible to see a clear rationale behind his choices. The "Life" had been written without the benefit of supporting documents, so it was, in many places factually inaccurate. When Clarendon substituted an account from the "Life" for one from the "History," he did not and could not always choose on the basis of accuracy. A good example occurs in Book III in connection with Strafford's impeachment. The "History" records that just as Pym retired after bringing the charge of impeachment to the House of Lords, Strafford entered and "was commanded to withdraw, and presently brought to the bar upon his knees, and from thence committed to prison" (3:note to 1). This account roughly agrees with contemporary evidence.[14] In the "Life," however, Clarendon had written a more elaborate version of the same incident. He chose to substitute it for the original. Now Clarendon has Strafford deliver a speech (3:11). We know that such was not the case: he asked to speak but was not allowed to do so. In a few instances the final *History* contains two contradictory accounts of the same event. The Militia Bill, for example, is mentioned in Book III (244-46) in a passage retained from the "History" and again in another section in Book IV (95-100) added from the "Life."

Much of the material which related principally to his own life, Clarendon did not include in the final *History*. When these sections were transferred into the *History*, Clarendon removed nearly all of these personal references, replacing them with indefinite pronouns or vague locutions. Such changes are small in number, but Firth correctly notes the theoretical problem they pose: "These alterations were designed to give an impersonal air to Clarendon's reminiscences and prevent any appearance of egotism, but the result is that in very many cases a vague periphrasis is substituted for a definite statement, so that the turns and changes of royalist politics become involved in unnecessary obscurity."[15]

The second stage in the preparation of the final *History* was more difficult. The original "History" ended with Book VII. All Clarendon now had was the manuscript "Life," but it was sketchy about many public matters which would have to be treated in a history of the period. Clarendon then was forced to write portions of a new narrative which would fill out and supplement the "Life" manuscript. All of this new material, which is at most extended fragments, was composed during the period between June 1671 and June 1672.

Not all of the new material added in this final period of composition is as factually inaccurate as much of the "Life" was. Among the material which Laurence brought to his father in 1671 were papers which Clarendon had been unable to use in writing the original "History." For his military narrative, Clarendon now had, among others, two accounts contributed by Sir Edward Walker: "His Maiesties happy progresse and successe from the 30th of March to the 23rd of November 1644" and "Brief Memorials of the unfortunate successe of his Maties army and affairs in the year 1645."[16] Similarly the sections dealing with attempted peace negotiations were also strengthened. For the new account of the French ambassador Montreuil's negotiations between Scotland and Charles II, Clarendon now had documentary evidence (10:23). For the new account of the treaty between the King and the Scots at Carisbrooke, signed December 1647, Clarendon had a copy of the document itself, for in places he exactly quotes it (10:161–67). Finally he added substantially to his account of the treaty between the king and Parliament on the Isle of Wight, explaining that his source here is a lengthy letter/diary which Charles I had written to his son the prince (11:189). The majority of the additions, however, concern the roles or actions of individuals. Clarendon's criticisms in this new material, especially in Books VIII and IX, which chronicle the progressive decay of the king's position, are among the sharpest in the *History*. Aware of this new tone,

Clarendon goes as far as to apologize for the way he handles this section and to emphasize that his criticisms are not based simply upon personal animosity (9:3).

What emerges from these new sections is a consistent emphasis on the way the king was destroyed by the "weakness and inadvertency" of a handful of men. The chief culprits in the West were Lord Goring and Sir Richard Greenville. Between Goring's arrogant demands and his negligence, one must conclude, Clarendon writes, "That if he had been confederate with the enemy, and been corrupted to betray the west, he could not have taken a more effectual way to do it" (9:101). He "[so] neglected and discouraged" his foot soldiers that they "ran away faster than they could be sent up to him"; his horse, in turn, executed "intolerable oppression, rapine, and violence" (9:47, 50), not on the enemy, but on the friendly countryside. Greenville's vice, on the other hand, was greed: "Though he suffered not his soldiers to plunder, yet he was in truth himself the greatest plunderer of this war" (9:62). Greenville was eventually imprisoned for refusing to serve under Hopton, and Goring fled to France.

The actions of Goring and Greenville were only a part of a larger pattern of flight and abandonment evident to Clarendon in the events of that year: the inexcusable flight of Prince Rupert and the Earl of Newcastle after the battle of Marston Moor (8:76–88); the mistaken flight of the King's cavalry at Naseby (9:40–41); the high rate of desertion under Goring (9:48); the rout and flight of Langdale's cavalry at the battle of Rowton Heath (9:119); the flight of Digby and Langdale after their fiasco in attempting to march to Scotland (9:123–27); and the final dissolution of the western army under Hopton (9:150). What Clarendon finds particularly reprehensible are the desertions by Goring, Rupert, Newcastle, Digby, and Langdale; they simply left their troops to "shift for themselves." Clarendon is right, of course, about the significance of such moves. Military coherence and discipline were quite weak in the seventeenth century. With a few notable exceptions, the success of a military operation depended upon the leadership abilities of a few men. If those men removed themselves from command, as they did in 1644–45, the king had no armies left.

By the time that Clarendon reached Book XII, the process of compiling the final *History* changed again. Generally the early books (I through VII) are composed mostly of material from the original "History," the middle books (VIII through XI) strike a rough balance between material transferred from the "Life" and new additions, and the final books (XII through XVI) are composed almost exclusively from material from the "Life." As we saw earlier, the further Clarendon wrote in his autobiography, the less personal material he included. Consequently, it was a simple matter to transfer the later portions of the "Life" directly into the final *History*. The *History* closes in exactly the same way as the final part of the "Life," with the return of Charles to London on his birthday, 29 May 1660.

The *History of the Rebellion* is then composed of materials written over a twenty-five year period.Clarendon worked quickly, producing within a year's time a complete manuscript draft. It is remarkable, given its composite nature, that the *History* emerges as the sustained, coherent work of art that it is. Having concentrated in this chapter on seeing the *History* as a series of disparate pieces fitted, sometimes casually, together to make a whole, it remains to examine the unity which resulted, a unity which makes the *History of the Rebellion* the first great English history and a lasting and significant work of art.

Chapter Three
The *History of the Rebellion* as History

The *History of the Rebellion* is important, in part, because it is a contemporary account of a turbulent period in English history. Clarendon's unique position during those years dictated that the *History*, regardless of its form or its excellence, would be an invaluable record of the English civil wars, the Interregnum, and the Restoration. Those years spawned many other contemporary accounts; none, however, approach in any way Clarendon's narrative. The *History of the Rebellion* marked the beginning of the tradition of English historical writing, a tradition which would include historians such as Gibbon, Carlyle, and Macaulay. It does so because of Clarendon's literary abilities and also because, from the outset, Clarendon conceived of his *History* as having a place in a tradition of history writing beginning with the Greek historians.

Clarendon was very conscious of previous models. In August 1647 he wrote to a friend: "That you may not think I am idle, I have read over Livy and Tacitus, and almost Tully's [Cicero's] works, and have written... near 300 large sheets of paper" (*Clarendon State Papers,* 2:375). Among the Clarendon manuscripts which survive are two collections of notes from his readings taken from 1646 to 1673. Included are extracts from a wide range of historians including Speed, Josephus, Plutarch, Livy, Grotius, Camden, Thucydides, and Bacon.[1] As the notes to Macray's edition of the *History* demonstrate, Clarendon's narrative is likewise sprinkled with allusions to or brief quotations from a range of classical historians including Thucydides, Plutarch, Tacitus, and Livy. Any detailed study of the influence of classical or Renaissance historians on Clarendon's narrative must lie outside of the scope of this book. It is possible, however, to isolate some general aspects of that influence, to define the intellectual milieu into which Clarendon's *History* falls. The

Renaissance historian was heir to two separate traditions: the first, an inheritance from the middle ages which was untouched by classical thought; the second, a discovery of the work of the great historians of Greece and Rome. The second was unquestionably the stronger and more important influence, but elements of the first linger on even in an historian such as Clarendon.

Medieval Historical Thought

The Middle Ages had a distinctly limited "sense of history," if any at all. Peter Burke offers a useful definition of the phrase. The "sense of history," he argues, includes three factors: a sense of anachronism, of the past as being different from the present; a sense of evidence, of weighing the relative reliability of sources; and a sense of causation;[2] the first two are basically missing in medieval historical thought. Medieval historical narratives were composites of material taken from sources without regard for their accuracy: "Men acted as if they believed that because something was written, it must be true; every 'author' was an 'authority' and what he wrote was 'authentic.'"[3] Myths were considered histories; documents were forged. The sense of causation is slightly more complicated: there were "causes" in medieval histories, but "they were not seen as problematic, as controversial, or in need of evidence." Burke continues: "Medieval histories lacked a middle ground between the ascription of motive to individuals, often done in a somewhat stereotyped way and then incorporated into the narrative without discussion, and extremely general interpretations of history in a theological manner." This limited sense of causation is reflected in the essentially annalistic structure of most medieval histories: "This framework tends to organise facts in a one-thing-after-another way; and so to exclude explanation. The favourite connective is not 'because' or 'as a result' but 'meanwhile.'"[4] When the Middle Ages produced something other than the annal, it tended to be a history of the world, a panoramic view of man since creation, a record of providential acts.

What is important for our purposes here are the medieval sense of causation and its sense of the purpose or value of history. If history revealed the hand of God, then obviously it had a didactic purpose. It becomes the business of the historian to point to events and to persons as moral examples. Such a providential view of cause and purpose survived into the Renaissance. For the Renaissance historian, the truths of history, writes Herschel Baker, "are paradigms of moral and political behavior, which, authenticated by famous men's experience, provide patterns that can shape our own response to perennially recurring situations."[5]

By the Renaissance, historians were increasingly aware of the limitations of such a view of causation. Robert Bolton in his *Hypercritica, or a rule of judgment for writing or reading our Historians* (ca. 1618) offered a typical criticism: "Christian authors while for their ease they shuffled up the reasons of events, in briefly referring all causes immediately to the Will of God, have generally neglected to inform their readers in the ordinary means of carriage in human affairs, and thereby maimed their narrations."[6]

To a certain extent Clarendon inherited some of this providential view of history. As we will see, causation in the *History* is variously explained. Although Clarendon documents personal causes at great length, nevertheless at a number of points in the narrative he makes reference to the hand and judgment of God. He structures particular episodes, as we will see in chapter 4, so as to reveal the hand of God. He employs providential language at various moments throughout the narrative.

Classical Historical Thought

The Renaissance rediscovery of the works of the great Greek and Roman historians had a tremendous impact on the nature and shape of historical writing. The classical historians provided new models. Their influence came in a number of areas, but several are particularly important for our purposes.

First, the classical historians provided a model for scope and subject matter. Rather than writing universal histories, histories of the whole world from creation, they tended to concentrate on particular periods of national development. More often than not, they wrote contemporary histories, concentrating on particular political and military events.[7] Second, the classical historians, particularly the Romans, elevated the writing of history to a literary art by applying the principles of rhetoric. They practiced their art with the same care and attention one would expect from an epic poet. Narratives were adorned with orations, characters were sketched, prose styles cultivated.

Third, the classical historians were deeply interested in causation and historical explanation. Why something happened was as important a question as what and how. Their interest in causation was, in part, an outgrowth of their view of the purpose and value of history. History recorded the actions of good and evil men; it enshrined their virtues or their villainy. Tacitus, in his *Annals,* sums it up in a way that applies to nearly all of the classical historians: "The first duty of history—to ensure that merit shall not lack its record and to hold before the vicious word and deed the terrors of posterity and infamy."[8] The immortality of the historical record was for the Romans the only reward or punishment there was. Correspondingly, the classical historians shared a common emphasis upon the individual—character became a key element in historical narratives.

Finally, since history records the actions of good and evil men, it has a didactic purpose: to provide the reader with examples of moral and, most especially, political behavior. Livy, in his *Ab Urbe Condita,* offers the classic and again typical view: "What chiefly makes the study of history wholesome and profitable is this, that you behold the lessons of every kind of experience set forth as on a conspicuous monument; from these you may choose for yourself and for your own state what to imitate, from these mark for avoidance what is shameful in the conception and shameful in the result."[9]

The *History of the Rebellion* in its shape, methods, and intentions was clearly influenced by its classical predecessors. Clarendon thought of himself as an English Thucydides or Tacitus; his view of the purpose of history was remarkably similar to theirs. In a letter dated 8 January 1647 he had noted, for example: "I take it to be no less the true end of history, to derive the eminency and virtue of those persons, who lived and acted in those times of which he writes, faithfully to posterity, than the counsels which were taken, or the actions which were done" (*Clarendon State Papers,* 2:328).

Machiavelli and Davila

Thus far we have traced two separate historical traditions. In the Renaissance the two came together. The classical historians had seen history as a storehouse of ethical examples, but they did not see it as a record of divine intervention. The medieval view of history, on the other hand, was completely theological. "Secular history," as F. Smith Fussner remarks, "was meaningful only as an illustration of divine providence."[10] This essentially Augustinian view of history began to lose its force in the Renaissance. In part this is attributable to the impact of the humanist historians, but it also owes much to the writings of a single man—Machiavelli.

Machiavelli's impact on historical thought parallels his impact on political theory, examined at some length in chapter 6. Basically, what Machiavelli did, in both *The Prince* and the *Discourses*, was to replace the medieval, theological view of society and its relationship to God with a pragmatic, secular view of political power. History and politics were severed from religion. The lessons of history were simply "axioms in Machiavelli's political science."[11] Machiavelli sought to describe or record what was or what worked rather than what should have been. One consequence was that the range of causation was expanded. Machiavelli's view in *The Prince* of the role of "Fortune" in man's life is a good example:

As I am well aware, many have believed and now believe human affairs so controlled by Fortune and by God that men with their prudence cannot manage them—yes, more, that men have no recourse against the world's variations. Such believers therefore decide that they need not sweat much over man's activities but can let Chance govern them. This belief has been the more firmly held in our times by reason of the great variations in affairs that we have seen in the past and now see every day beyond all human prediction. Thinking on these variations, I myself now and then incline in some respects to their belief. Nonetheless, in order not to annul our free will, I judge it true that Fortune may be mistress of one half our actions but that she leaves the other half, or almost, under our control.[12]

Clarendon was clearly influenced by Machiavelli's view of the value of history for rulers. In reading the *Discourses* he noted:

Machiavelli to extoll his owne excellent judgement, and insight in History, would persuade men to believe that the reason why so many mischieves befall States, is because their governours have not observed the same mischieves heretofore, in story and therefor by their wisdomes prevented, for if they had, he sayes, it would be easy by examining the thinges that are past, to foresee the future in any Commonwealth. And if all History were written by as wise men as Machiavell, and the true grounds and originalls of all difficulties to the State observed, and then remedyed, surely there needs little more wisdom for government, than a dispassionate and sober perusall of those Storyes; but as accounts of that nature are commonly denyed unto us, we rather know the misfortunes than the faults of our Auncestors, and are only informed into what inconveniences they have fallen, not by what errors they befell them.[13]

One other Renaissance historian is worth singling out here. Enrico Caterino Davila's *Storia delle guerre civili di Francia* appeared in an English edition, *The Historie of the Civill Warres of France*, in 1647. Part of the significance of Davila lies in his detailed explanations of the hidden causes of those wars. Discovering the truth, Davila notes, is difficult:

The Civill Warres ... though on the one side they contain great Actions and famous Enterprizes, that may serve for excellent lessons to those that maturely consider them; yet on the other side, they are so confused and intangled in their own revolutions, that the reasons of many businesses doe not appear, the counsels of many determinations are not rightly comprehended, and an infinite number of things not at all understood through the partiality of private Interests, which under divers pretences hath obscured the truth of them.[14]

Both royalists and parliamentarians saw Davila's *Historie* as providing a model for the rebellion in England. The prefatory statement "To the Reader" in the 1678 edition clearly establishes the relationship:

Nor hath He [Davila] wanted a due value here, for, our late King [Charles I] ... by whose Command, at Oxford, this Translation was Continued and Finished (though not begun) read it there, with such eagerness, that no Diligence could Write it out faire, so fast as he daily called for it, wishing he had had it some years sooner, out of a Beliefe, that being forewarned thereby, He might have prevented many of those Mischiefs we then groaned under; and which the Grand Contrivers of them, had drawn from this Original, as Spiders do Poison from the most wholsome Plants. The Truth is, their Swords had already Transcribed it in English Blood, before this Pen had done it in English Inke.[15]

Clarendon was familiar with Davila's *Historie*; he praised Davila's character sketches of the actors in his narrative. Even more revealing are Clarendon's remarks in a letter to the Earl of Bristol, dated 1 February 1647, likening his work to Davila's: "And therefore you will find D'Avila (who, I think, hath written as our's should be written, and from whence no question our Gamesters learnt much of their play) insert the declarations of both sides in the main body of the story, as the foundations upon which all that was after done, was built" (*Clarendon State Papers*, 2:334).

The Historian's Qualifications and Purpose

Part of Clarendon's fascination with Machiavelli and Davila surely lay in their use of history as a source of political wisdom. When he began his original "History," Clarendon stressed its pragmatic value. Correspondingly, it was because he was an experienced advisor to the king who personally knew the men involved that he felt qualified to undertake his "History" in the first place. His qualifications for the job were practical and based upon his experience: "I may not be thought altogether an incompetent person for this communication, having been present as a member of Parliament in those councils before and till the breaking out of the Rebellion, and having since had the honour to be near two great kings in some trust" (1:3).

In an undated essay "On an Active and on a Contemplative Life," Clarendon expanded on his view of the historian. He writes: "There was never yet a good History written but by Men conversant in Business, and of the best and most liberal Education." History, he continues,

is not a Collection of Records, or an Admission to the View and Perusal of the most secret Letters and Acts of State, (though they are great and necessary Contributions) which can enable a Man to write a History, if there be an Absence of that Genius and Spirit and Soul of an Historian, which is contracted by the Knowledge and Course and Method of Business, and by Conversation and Familiarity in the Inside of Courts, and the most active and eminent Persons in the Government. (*Tracts*, 180)

Any person who hopes to compile "the best and most useful" history of his time must therefore be a man of "action" and of experience. He cites Davila and Guido Bentivoglio, author of *The compleat history of the warrs of Flanders* (English translation 1654), as models. They succeed, he feels, because "commonly the greatest Persons they have occasion to mention were very well known to them both, which makes their Characters always very lively" (*Tracts*, 180). On the other hand, Hugo Grotius failed or rather disappoints: "His History ... did not satisfy the Expectation the world had of it, neither in the Life and Spirit of it, nor in the clear Description of the Councils upon which great Enterprizes were undertaken, nor the Conduct of those Enterprizes, with a lively Representation of Persons and Actions" (*Tracts*, 181). England's history had never been adequately recorded, he continues, in part because her historians had lacked the necessary qualifications:

What I say of the different Value of Histories, according to the Qualifications of the Persons who write them, no doubt hath been the Reason that so small, if any Part of our own is tolerably set out: for I cannot reckon any History or Relation, of how long or short Time soever, performed in any Degree of Perfection, when as important, or at least very important Particulars are totally left out as those which are inserted ... which proceeds from the want of Encouragement of fit Persons, who know how to call for Contributions ... and are themselves conversant with the universal Transactions of *Christendom* during that time of which they write. (*Tracts*, 181–82)

History, for Clarendon, was a way of understanding the present and the future in terms of the past. When he first began work on the original "History," he intended his historical narrative to be an instructive guide to past mistakes, and, by implication, to future political conduct. By isolating the errors which led to the rebellion, he would be making a valuable contribution to practical politics.

The *History* as a "manual of advice" is nowhere more evident than in Clarendon's comments on the qualifications and functions of a privy councillor in Book III. In their proceedings against Strafford in 1640, Parliament got Charles's consent "for the examining upon oath [of] Privy Councillors upon such matters as had passed at the Council-table" (3:45). The implications of such a move were disastrous for it "banished for ever all future freedom from that board and those persons from whence his majesty was to expect advice in his greatest straits; all men satisfying themselves that they were no more obliged to deliver their opinions there freely, when they might be impeached in another place for so doing" (3:47). Charles went even further, calling to his council eight members of the parliamentary opposition. Such an action prompts from Clarendon a lengthy discourse on the qualifications necessary in a privy councillor: he must, first, be "fixed to monarchic grounds, the preservation and upholding whereof is the chief end of such a Council" and, second, he must believe that in order to function properly "there [must be] a dignity, a freedom, a jurisdiction, most essential to be preserved in and to that place" (3:51).

The importance of "advisors" in the monarchy, for Clarendon, lies in two areas. First, in the early stage of the rebellion parliamentary criticism was directed not toward Charles himself, but toward those "evil councillors" who were supposedly at fault. At least in the beginning, the monarch was above direct criticism. Even Clarendon is careful to attribute Charles's errors to the advice he received from others rather than to his own decisions, although at a number of points in the narrative we can sense his disapproval of the king's actions. Second, as we will see with reference to causation in the narrative, Clarendon traced the origins of the rebellion to personal causes rather than to political, economic, or religious forces. For Clarendon individuals determined the course of history. Consequently, those in power must act dispassionately and responsibly. The danger, most clearly exemplified in the digression concerning the Duke of Buckingham, was that policies and actions were often determined or initiated by those totally unqualified to do so. The king could be, and was, influenced by "favorites" rather than by responsible advisors. A King, Clarendon continues, "is not thought a great monarch when he follows the reins of his own reason and appetite, but when, for the informing his reason and guiding his actions, he uses the service, industry, and faculties of the wisest men" (3:53). Such digressions reveal the extent to which certain portions of the *History* were intended to embody political wisdom.

This is not to imply, however, that the *History*, in either its original or final form, was ever intended as just a "manual of advice" for the king. Two other didactic intentions are clearly discernible. The first, discussed at some length in chapter 5, is Clarendon's desire to "memoralize" those who sacrificed their fortunes and lives for the monarchy. The second was to reveal to "posterity" the "real" pattern which was evident in the turmoil, the "real" reasons why the rebellion occurred. Here Clarendon is particularly anxious to refute any interpretation which saw the "rebellion" as a providential act.

Such a view—that God was acting in history to remove a tyrant and to establish the Millennium—was a fairly common and powerful idea in England in the 1640s. Clarendon acknowledged the "hand and judgment of God" (2:2) in the initiating events, but any divine intervention was not caused by disapproval of either Charles or the monarchy. Charles, Clarendon writes, was "of the most harmless disposition and the most exemplar piety, the greatest example of sobriety, chastity, and mercy, that any prince hath been endued with" (1:163). In part what Clarendon is reacting to is the seventeenth-century Puritan providential reading of history by which England, like Israel, was a chosen nation and so was destined to break the natural cyclical pattern of rise and fall because of God's special providential dispensation. The Milliennium before the second actual coming of Christ, they believed, was near at hand. If the English people and especially the English Parliament were capable of seizing the opportunity, the perfect reformation could be achieved within history. History, as a result, was read for confirmation and for prediction. For the English Puritans, of course, the crisis never came and prediction failed with the failure of the revolution, with the growing oppressiveness of Parliament, and finally with the restoration of Charles II. Clarendon's interpretation of history counters such a view. It was, after all, for Clarendon, a "rebellion" rather than a "revolution."

Causation

One thing that distinguishes a history from a simple chronicle is the element of causation. In a history events are seen in relation to one another: events initiate, contribute to, or resolve a sequence. Every history reflects either implicitly or explicitly a theory of causation. As we have seen, for medieval and early renaissance historians, causation was providential; history revealed the hand of God at work. By the late Renaissance, historians began increasingly to emphasize secondary causes, the "freely willed" actions of men. Even then, theories of causation tended, by modern standards, to be fairly limited. It was not until the nineteenth and twentieth centuries that historians began to see, for example, social or economic forces as primary causative principles.[16]

We might object to the theory of causation that an historian uses to "explain" a story. It might seem to us as either "wrong" or as inadequate. Or we might object to the lack of an explicit, detailed theory of causation, feeling that the historian has not sufficiently explained causes. Clarendon's *History* has been criticized on both accounts. Firth, for example, felt that Clarendon missed the "real" cause of the revolution: "Motives which influenced masses of men escape his appreciation, and the *History of the Rebellion* is accordingly an account of the Puritan Revolution which is unintelligible because the part played by Puritanism is misunderstood or omitted altogether."[17] Sir James Stephen, on the other hand, went even further:

Any book with the faintest pretensions to rise above the rank of a collection of dates would contain some view as to the general causes of the civil wars—some account of the principles represented by the two contending parties, and of the degree in which those principles rose out of, or were suggested by, the ancient institutions of the country.... Their total absence, and the absence of any notion of the very possibility of making them... [makes] the story unintelligible. Why, the reader asks again and again, did a quiet, orderly, loyal people rush into civil war? The only explanation suggested by Clarendon is that they waxed fat and kicked, that, being puffed up by peace and prosperity, they took to cutting each other's throats—a simply childish notion.[18]

The principal theory of causation which underlies the *History of Rebellion* attributes the rebellion to those in power—both the king's advisors and military officers and the "contrivers of the mischief" (4:36) in Parliament. Clarendon does not see a consistent thread or principle running through events; he does not see a consistent pattern of motivation among the actors in his narrative. Nor did he see it as being historically inevitable: "I am not so sharp-sighted as those who have discerned this rebellion contriving from, if not before, the death of Queen Elizabeth, and fomented by several Princes and great ministers of state in Christendom to the time that it brake out" (1:4). Nor was the rebellion the result of a conspiracy or plot:

Neither do I look so far back as believing the design to be so long since formed; (they who have observed the several accidents, not capable of being contrived, which have contributed to the several successes, and do know the persons who have been the grand instruments of this change, of whom there have not been any four of familiarity and trust with each other, will easily absolve them from so much industry and foresight in their mischief. (1:4)

Clarendon acknowledged that Parliament did have some legitimate grievances which had accumulated over the years during which Charles did not summon a Parliament; he did acknowledge royalist error. Such things are, as we saw in chapter 2, catalogued at length in Books I and II of the *History*. Nevertheless, for Clarendon the rebellion was, in a very real sense, a sudden and avoidable disruption. The period from 1629 to 1640, the interval of personal rule, was, Clarendon asserts, a time of peace and prosperity: "All his majesty's dominions ... enjoyed the greatest calm and the fullest measure of felicity that any people in any age for so long time together have been blessed with" (1:159). In comparison, neither the times of Queen Elizabeth (1558–1603) nor those of King James

(1603-1624) were as calm and tranquil. Ironically, it was the prosperity that provided the climate in which the seeds of the rebellion could grow:

But all these blessings could but enable, not compel, us to be happy: we wanted that sense, acknowledgment, and value of our own happiness.... The Court full of excess, idleness and luxury, and the country full of pride, mutiny and discontent; every man more troubled and perplexed at that they called the violation of one law, than delighted or pleased with the observation of all the rest of the charter: never imputing the increase of their receipts, revenue and plenty to the wisdom, virture and merit of the Crown, but objecting every little trivial imposition to the exorbitancy and tyranny of the government. (1:164)

The "immediate finger and wrath of God" can be seen in "these perplexities and distractions" but it attends a kingdom and a people "swoln with long plenty, pride, and excess" (1:2). The nation was "ripe and prepared for destruction" (1:2), yet the cause was not divine judgment, but individual failings: "The pride of this man, and the popularity of that; the levity of one, and the morosity of another; the excess of the court in the greatest want, and the parsimony and retention of the country in the greatest plenty; the spirit of craft and subtlety in some, and the rude and unpolished integrity of others, too much despising craft or art" (1:4). Throughout the *History*, Clarendon sees personal causes. This, in part, accounts for his interest in character. The history of the rebellion was not a "universal corruption of the hearts of the whole nation [that] had brought forth those lamentable effects," but rather "the folly and the frowardness... the weakness and the wilfulness, the pride and the passion, of particular persons" (9:2).

The principle of causation is not, however, always consistent in the *History*. The rebellion and the events that led up to it origi- nated for Clarendon in a series of mistakes and willful actions taken by individual men—both those who favored and those who opposed the king. On the other hand, acts of deliverance, moments of victory, and the Restoration itself are seen by Clarendon as providential. The extent to which Clarendon structures particular episodes as acts of God and uses providential language is examined in some detail in chapter 4. Clearly, of course, there was no other way that Clarendon could have "read" the historical record.

Sources

When Clarendon first began work on the original "History" in 1646, he realized that his narrative must be based upon more than just his own experience and memory; otherwise, large portions of the story of the rebellion would remain untold. He had been a member of Parliament until he joined the king in 1642; he had been author of nearly all of the king's propaganda efforts during the "paper skirmish" years. As one might expect, these portions of the narrative are particularly detailed. On the other hand, his knowledge about other matters was often quite limited. From October 1642 to March 1645 he had, for example, remained in Oxford, removed from any firsthand experience of the military conduct of the war. Events in Scotland and Ireland, or even in London itself, could only be related through the assistance of others.

To supplement the "few pamphlets and diurnals" (*Clarendon State Papers,* 2:385) he had on hand, he turned to a wide range of correspondents. In the earliest reference to his work on the "History," he wrote to Lord Widdrington on 5 August 1646: "I have not been at too immoderate a distance (if that were qualification enough) from the publick agitations, to venture upon this relation; yet the scene of action lying in so many several places, a much wiser and more conversant person than myself must desist from this work, except others assist him, by communicating what hath been transacted in their several spheres" (*Clarendon State Papers,* 2:246). He then goes on to request specific information about "affairs" in the North of England. Despite his efforts, however, contributions were slow in coming. On 15 November, some eight months after he began writing and by the time he was already as far as Book IV, he wrote to Lord Cottington:

I have not had so good luck, having not been able yet to procure the
contribution of one diurnal towards my great Volume: but now you and
Mr. Secretary [Nicholas] are so near me, I look for notable supplies.
(*Clarendon State Papers,* 2: 292)

The same day he wrote to Nicholas:

You are obliged to give me your advertisements, and send me those
informations of all kinds, with which you can plentifully supply me. If I
had my own papers which I left in Oxford, they would help me. I pray
bethink yourself of the business of Ireland; and whatever you have of it, or
can recollect upon your memory, send to me. I have sent to London for
many papers, books, and some records, which I have great hope of
obtaining; and if I can settle a safe correspondence with that opulent city,
all will be well. (*Clarendon State Papers,* 2:289)

In a later letter to Nicholas, he chidingly reiterated his requests, this
time more specifically:

I desyre you will by all your diligence, intercourse, and dexterity, procure
such materials for me, for my history, as you know necessary; which I take
to be so much your work, that if you fail in it, I will put marginal notes into
the history, that shall reproach you for want of contribution, By you, that
is, by your care, I must be supplied with all the acts of countenance and
confederacy which have passed from France, Holland, Spain, in favour of
the rogues in England; from you I must have all the passages in the war,
which have only been remembered by Sir Edmund Walker, from whom
you must recover them, besides your own memorials of Ireland &c.
(*Clarendon State Papers,* 2:318)

For what were the first five books of the original "History,"
Clarendon had few problems. He could write about the actions in
Parliament until 1642; he could relate in great detail the paper
propaganda battle that followed. It was not until he reached the war
years that he really needed contributions from others. His coverage
for those years depended upon the success he had in securing such
information. Some actions are treated in great detail; others are
barely mentioned or are omitted completely. In some instances it is

possible to establish in some detail the extent to which portions of the narrative are derived from contributions secured from others. For example, Hyde's account of events in the West during the first war is based on a series of documents provided by Sir Ralph Hopton and Colonel Slingsby, an officer under Hopton. These documents include three separate narratives by Hopton—an account of affairs in the West from September 1642 to June 1643; another covering the period from June 1643 until the capture of Bristol by Prince Rupert on 26 July 1643; and a third recounting the battle of Alresford, 29 March 1644—and three by Slingsby—an account of the battle of Lansdown, 5 July 1643, and of Roundway, 13 July 1643; another on the siege of Bristol; and a third on the battle of Alresford.[19] For these sections of the *History* Clarendon made extensive use of two of Hopton's narratives, using, as Firth noted, both factual details and, at times, Hopton's phraseology. Firth observes: "Hyde does not hesitate to abridge Hopton freely, and omits many unimportant incidents. He inserts with equal freedom general reflexions upon the causes or consequences of particular events, and upon the characters of the persons mentioned.[20]

The sections derived from Hopton's accounts are among the clearest examples there are of Clarendon's use of source material. Among the manuscripts preserved in the collection of Clarendon papers at the Bodleian Library, Oxford, there are others of which he seems to have made some use. These include an anonymous account of the battle of Hopton Heath, 19 March 1643;[21] accounts of the siege and surrender of Donnington Castle and of Winchester;[22] and a relation by Joseph Jane of the state of the parties in Cornwall from the commencement of the rebellion and the campaigns there until Sir Richard Greenville's arrival.[23] There are two other summaries of military events of the period as well: one covers the interval from June 1642 through March 1648,[24] and the other is four pages of notes in Clarendon's own handwriting on the movements of the Marquis of Newcastle, Sir Thomas Glenham, and the Scots army from 1642 through the surrender of York.[25]

In the same collection there are other manuscripts which, for one reason or another, were not used. Some reached Clarendon too late to be used in the original "History." Sir Hugh Cholmley, the former governor of Scarborough, sent three narratives: "Memorials touching Scarborough" (telling of his surrender of it to the queen); "Memorial touching the battle of York [Marston Moor]"; and "Some observations and Memorials touching the Hothams" (Sir John Hotham and his son, relating their intrigue with the Earl of Newcastle and their subsequent execution, 1 and 2 January 1645).[26] These apparently reached Clarendon sometime in 1648. Other accounts include a narrative of the military proceedings in the North from 1641 to 1645 inclusive, concentrating on those which involved the Marquis of Newcastle and the town of Newcastle;[27] Lord Byron's account of the first battle of Newbury, 20 September 1643;[28] a brief account of the siege of Lyme in 1644;[29] Prince Rupert's journal in England, 5 September 1642 to 4 July 1646—received from the Prince of Wales in early April 1648;[30] and two by Sir Edward Walker, "His Majesties happy progresse and successe from the 30th of March to the 23rd of November 1644" and "Brief Memorials of the unfortunate success of his Maties army and affairs in the year 1645."[31] These last two were used, however, when Clarendon completed the final *History* in 1670.

There may have been other manuscript contributions which have not survived. In addition to these specific documents, Clarendon would have had other secondhand sources of information. Based as he was in Oxford from 1642 to 1645, he would have had access to the reports and letters sent in from the king's armies throughout England. Much of this material was also published in the *Mercurius Aulicus*, a weekly royalist newspaper. Firth speculates, quite reasonably, that Clarendon might well have had some issues of this newspaper with him in Jersey in 1646.[32]

In the sections of the *History* derived from the original "History," we can see Clarendon attempting to work around the problems caused by inadequate information. In Book VII, for example, there is a long and detailed account of the progress of the war in the West including the battles of Stratton, Chewton Mendip, Lansdown, and Roundway Down. Here Clarendon had relied on the narratives supplied by Hopton supplementing these with information from unknown sources. But having finished with Roundway

Down, he had originally planned an account of the progress of the king's army in the North under the Earl of Newcastle. He had apparently intended a narrative of some length, announcing first that Newcastle's actions there

> were so prosperous, and so full of notable accidents, that they deserve a history apart; and therefore I shall only insert such of them in this place [as] were most signal, and which had the greatest influence upon the series of the greatest affairs. (7:note to 121)

The narrative breaks off, though, after only a few more lines; the rest of the manuscript page and the next one were left blank apparently to be finished whenever the contribution from Newcastle arrived. Clarendon tried repeatedly to get Newcastle's assistance, but in the end, he was forced to give up.[33]

During the two later periods of composition—the "Life" in 1668 to 1670 and the final *History* in 1671 to 1672—Clarendon did not have access to anywhere near a comparable amount of source material. Indeed, during the years that he worked on the "Life" he apparently had almost nothing but his memory. The value of the *History* as a source of factual information about the events of the period depends upon whether the particular section in question was a part of the original "History" or "Life" or was composed when the two were worked together to make the final *History*. In the "Life" he tended to avoid accounts about which he had no personal knowledge. Typically, for example, he summarized events, dismissing them as "fitter subjects for the history of that time than for this narration."

Despite such dismissals, though, Clarendon's choices in the "Life" were often influenced more by his lack of information than by his feelings that military actions had no role in a memoir such as he was writing. When he had some direct knowledge of an event, he tended to include it, whether it was significant in the course of the war or relevant in some way to his own life. Thus, for example, while he wrote one paragraph on the battle with Waller's forces at Cropredy (8:note to 73); another on the surrender of Essex's foot soldiers in Cornwall (8:note to 96); just mentioned the crucial battle at Marston-Moor (8:note to 75); he also included an extended account of the plans of Montrose and Antrim to begin a military diversion in Scotland (8:261-79)—a plan hatched in Oxford where Clarendon was staying at the time.

The instances where Clarendon had source material at hand when he was working on the "Life" are few indeed. He did write a long account of the peace negotiations at Uxbridge in January 1645 (8:209-41, 243, 249-54), but he had been responsible for preparing all of the written papers which passed between the two sides. The only other place that we can clearly establish that Clarendon did have documentary evidence is in the elaborate relation of the seizure and subsequent surrender of Pontefract Castle (11:115-26). The event hardly warrants such coverage and has nothing to do with Clarendon's life, but it is derived from an anonymous manuscript now in the Bodleian collection.[34]

Clarendon was always aware of the inadequacies of his narrative and often indicated his later intentions. As we saw in chapter 2, he never finished Part II of the "Life" because he had already written an account of that period during his first exile in Jersey. What he did was to indicate that he would rework that original manuscript and then insert it into the "Life." Similarly, he was not pleased with the detail which he had included in his account of the embassy to Spain in 1649. Again he added a note to the manuscript indicating that whenever he secured his papers, he intended to make changes and additions.[35]

When his son Laurence visited in June 1671, he brought along the manuscript of the original "History" and a number of other documents. Correspondingly, sections of the *History* written during this final stage of composition can have a much greater accuracy than material written for the "Life." For the first seven books Clarendon had, between the original "History" and the "Life," a fairly complete account. It was only after Book VIII that he was forced to write new sections to supplement what was often a spotty account in the "Life." Consequently it is in these later books that we can see Clarendon's use of additional source material.

Clarendon begins Book VIII by finishing the account of Hopton's campaign during the winter of 1643 which he had left unfinished in 1646. He now had Hopton's papers and he used these as the basis for a new narrative (8:1–17). He canceled the paragraph on the battle of Cropredy Bridge which he had written for the "Life" and now substituted a new, longer and more accurate account, working now from one of Edward Walker's accounts. In Book IX Clarendon integrated the two pieces of manuscript which he had completed on Jersey but never used—'the "westerne businesse" account and the fragment dealing with the prince's Council and the Duke of Hamilton. He used the first for 102 sections of a total of 178 in Book IX; the second for 8 sections.

In Books IX and X Clarendon added an account of the efforts of Montreuil, sent from France to negotiate a peace between the Scots and Charles, explaining the source of new information: "Since I have in my hands all the original letters which passed from him to the King, and the King's answers and directions thereupon, or such authentic copies thereof as have been by myself examined with the originals" (10:23).[36] Similarly he added as well a new account of the treaty between the king and the Scots at Carisbrooke, signed 26 December 1647 on the Isle of Wight. Here, as Firth has pointed out, Clarendon must have had a copy of the treaty, for his summary is not only accurate but in places exactly quotes the treaty.[37]

In Book XI Clarendon made use of Marmaduke Langdale's narrative of the battle of Preston (11:73–77) and Philip Musgrave's relation concerning the actions of his group of royalists in the north (11:16, 18, 52–54, 92–96).[38] He added as well to his account of the treaty between the king and Parliament on the Isle of Wight, begun in September 1648, explaining that his source was a letter/diary which Charles I had kept for his son.[39] The final two books also show evidence of Clarendon's use of source material. There is a good summary of the naval successes of the English fleet in the West Indies in Book XV and an accurate account of Cromwell's speeches to his first parliament and his speech accepting the Humble Petition and Advice. In Book XVI there is a fairly long and quite accurate account of the Army's petition of 6 April 1659, about the "good old cause," their subsequent declaration of 6 May inviting the Long Parliament to reassemble, and Richard's resignation and submission to Parliament. This whole section is so accurate that

Firth feels that Clarendon had at hand some form of printed evidence.[40]

As this section on sources indicates, Clarendon, throughout the three stages of composition, made every attempt possible to secure the fullest and most accurate information for his *History*. What he sought from others were accounts of particular actions in which he himself played no part. In a sense, though, his attempts reveal his particular bias in the *History*. That is, the record that needed to be filled out, for Clarendon, was the military record. It was not necessary to supplement his own knowledge of Parliament's activities or the motivations of the Parliamentarian opposition. Similarly, he apparently made no attempt to secure information about any aspect of the religious issues involved. Clarendon's view of the "causes" for the "rebellion," in other words, predetermined the nature of the information which he felt was necessary to complete his story.

What is important about the *History of the Rebellion* is not its factual accuracy or its completeness. Every history is at best a selective record and a consciously or unconsciously biased one. Rather what is important is Clarendon's sustained interpretation of events as he constructs and shapes his narrative to tell a story. Clarendon consciously conceived of his *History* as having a place in a tradition of history writing stretching from Thucydides to his own time. He had the experience, the political wisdom, the capacity for insight and interpretation, the impartiality necessary in a great historian. What he also had, as we will see in the next chapter, was the ability to fashion his *History* into a great work of art as well.

Chapter Four
The *History of the Rebellion* as Literature

At the start of his essay "Clio, A Muse," George Macaulay Trevelyan laments the increasing separation between history and literature: "Two generations back, history was a part of our national literature, written by persons moving at large in the world of letters or politics." Since then, he continues, history has been "proclaimed a 'science' for specialists, not 'literature' for the common reader of books." He traces the English tradition of regarding history as "a part of the national literature" which was "meant for the education and delight of all who read books" back to Clarendon's *History of the Rebellion.*[1] Trevelyan's remarks were written early in this century, and since then the gap between the two has, if anything, increased. Literary criticism has increasingly come to apply the term "literature" to what we would call works of "fiction" rather than works of "fact." Indeed, history, in the sense of works such as Clarendon's *History of the Rebellion*, Gibbon's *Decline and Fall of the Roman Empire*, or Macaulay's *History of England*, have no place today in the curriculum of English literature. Our critical methods of analysis and interpretation seem totally unsuited for historical works.

Yet at the same time that literary critics have increasingly divorced history from literature, historians have increasingly become aware of the links which bind the two, or, to use Hayden White's phrase, of the "historical text as literary artifact."[2] White's remarks on the literary or fictive aspects of historical narratives offer the literary critic a way to bridge the gap which now separates literary analysis and historical texts.

Historical narratives, White asserts, are "verbal fictions, the contents of which are as much invented as found and the forms of which have more in common with their counterparts in literature

67

than they have with those in the sciences."[3] The historian makes
sense out of the mass of facts that is the historical record by
transforming them or arranging them into a story. "No given set of
casually recorded historical events in themselves constitute a story;
the most that they offer to the historian are story elements." The
process of converting facts into stories is, White asserts, a fiction-
making operation: "The events are made into a story by the
suppression or subordination of certain of them and the highlight-
ing of others, by characterization, motific repetition, variation of
tone and point of view, alternative descriptive strategies, and the
like—in short, all of the techniques that we would normally expect
to find in the emplotment of a novel or a play."[4]

As powerfully suggestive as White's views are, Clarendon's
History of the Rebellion presents some fairly unique and disturb-
ing problems for the literary critic. For one thing, the *History*
violates the two fundamental assumptions that any critic would
have about a literary work: first that it would have integrity in the
sense that the work reflects a consistency of purpose and, second,
that its parts would be properly subordinated to the "end" toward
which the whole is aimed. Because the *History* resulted from fusing
together two separate works which had distinctively different
intentions and methods, its composition was not governed by a
sustained, consistent purpose. Questions about the relationships
between parts and whole are correspondingly difficult to answer.
And these are not the only problems. The *History* as we read it
today is essentially a first-draft version. It took Clarendon about a
year to combine the "History" and "Life," adding some new material as he went. He never had the opportunity to work through the
final transcript to eliminate inconsistencies, tighten transitions,
make structural changes or stylistic revisions. As a result, many
careless errors which Clarendon made in his haste are preserved as
if they represented his final intentions. And finally, not even
Macray's edition, careful as it is, always perserves Clarendon's
original sentence and paragraph divisions.

For the literary critic such a range of problems is staggering.
Consequently, little attention has been paid to the *History* as a
whole. It is most frequently seen as two or three separate pieces. To
some extent such a separation is both necessary and important,

especially for the historian interested in assessing the accuracy of Clarendon's account of a particular event. Despite its textual difficulties, despite its final patchwork nature by literary standards, the *History of the Rebellion* is a coherent work of art. It does have a beginning, middle, and an end. It does have unifying concerns; it does rest upon a consistent set of values. And, most importantly, it does exhibit the same fundamental literary elements that we expect to find in any work of literature. Using some of the theoretical framework provided by White, it is possible to examine the *History* in the same way that we would any "verbal fiction."

Plot

A chronicle is simply a chronological record of events—an "open-ended" list. It can begin anywhere and end anywhere. There is no causality holding the events together; no shape or story; no beginning. middle, and end. Out of that string of events, the historian shapes a story. Events are seen as "initiating" or "contributing to" or "resolving" a pattern of action. As White remarks: "the historian arranges the events in the chronicle into a hierarchy of significance by assigning events different functions as story elements in such a way as to disclose the formal coherence of a whole set of events considered as a comprehensible process with a discernible beginning, middle, and end."[5]

Using literary terminology, we would say that the historian turns a chronicle into a story by constructing a plot. Plot in a literary work can be defined as the selection and arrangement or patterning of events into a causal and inevitable sequence predetermined by the writer.[6] Superficially at least, the writer of fiction, writing about what could be rather than about what was, has an infinitely greater freedom in constructing plot than does the writer of history. The fiction writer can "invent," but the historian is bound to the "truth" of what was. Historians do not "invent," rather they "discover" plot or story in the "facts" that have been amassed. The implication is that the plot the historian constructs has a validity or truth that is verified by and arises out of the "facts."

We do know, however, that historians do not always see the same plot configurations in the same series of events. If they did, there would be no conflicting interpretations. In fact, of course, historians construct disparate accounts of the same action. In the instance of the English civil wars, one historian selects evidence which casts those wars as a religious revolution, another as a constitutional conflict, a third as a class struggle. Their version of the "facts"—their selectivity and arrangement of them—conforms to the story that they see contained within the evidence. This is so because the difference between the historian and the fiction writer is not as great as it seems, for, to use White's word, histories are "emplotted" in the same ways that fictions are. No history embraces all of the facts; no history is impartial. All histories are interpretative; otherwise, they simply remain chronicles. What the historian does is to select events and arrange them into a particular pattern which seems to provide the most acceptable explanation of what happened. In the process some events are ignored, some are emphasized, some are subordinated—all in the interest of endowing, as White observes, "the set of historical events...with a meaning of a particular kind."[7] We see in events, in a sense, whatever we are disposed to see. It does not depend upon our knowledge of the "facts" but upon our predisposition to select and arrange those facts in a particular, predetermined order which seems to us to "best fit" the facts.

As we saw in the previous chapter, Clarendon's *History of the Rebellion* is an interpretive work. Clarendon seeks to explain why the rebellion happened. His account is limited not just by his difficulties in securing information, but also by the particular story that he sees revealed in the events. The extent to which Clarendon emplotted his narrative in particular configurations is evident in both specific episodes within the narrative and in the structure of the *History* as a whole.

Clarendon's account of the restoration of Charles II is a particularly revealing example of "emplotment." The opening sections of Book XVI of the *History*, the final book, cover the period from Richard Cromwell's succession through his resignation. Throughout all of this, Clarendon repeatedly emphasizes, prospects for a restoration appeared extremely bleak, so bleak that only a miracle could effect it:

And in this state of despair the King's condition was concluded to be at the end of March 1660; and though his majesty, and those few intrusted by him, had reason to believe that God would be more propitious to him, from some great alterations in England, yet such imagination was so looked upon as mere dotage that the King thought not fit to communicate the hopes he had, but left all men to cast about for themselves, till they were awakened and confounded by such a prodigious act of Providence as he hath scarce vouchsafed to any nation, since he led his own chosen people through the Red Sea. (16:77)

The sudden change of events was, Clarendon emphasizes, totally unexpected. The struggles of Parliament, Lambert, the army, and the eventual establishment of the Committee of Safety to replace Parliament as a governing body brought General Monck, with his army, from Scotland to demand the reconvening of Parliament. Clarendon's character sketch of Monck leaves little doubt about his own attitudes toward the man who would be the instrument through which Charles was restored. Monck's most distinctive characteristics, for Clarendon, were his greed and his stupidity. Clarendon makes it quite clear that Monck's initial contribution to Charles's restoration was unintentional and that he imagined nothing more than "his own profit and greatness under the establishment of its [Parliament's] government" (16:101). The restoration, or as Clarendon remarks, the "resurrection" of Parliament, dashed royalist hopes again:

It may be justly said, and transmitted as a truth to posterity, that there was not one man who bore a part in these changes and giddy revolutions who had the least purpose or thought to contribute to the King's restoration, or who wished well to his interest; they who did so being so totally suppressed and dispirited, that they were only at gaze what light might break out of this darkness, and what order Providence might produce out of this confusion. (16:111)

Clarendon configures the restoration as a miracle—a providential act. It is surprising that a political analyst such as he would have minimized the more rational aspects of the restoration. He was, after all, the chief architect of the political and propagandistic

moves that Charles II made. He was aware of the more simple force
of political inevitability, that England functioned best (and almost
only) under the rule of a single central figure. That when that figure
was removed only Charles II was strong enough to assume control,
and that Charles's strength was neither political or military but
rather was inherent in the monarchical system. There is abundant
evidence in Clarendon's correspondence from the time to demonstrate the political complexity of the restoration and Clarendon's
crucial role in that process. All of this, though, is ignored by
Clarendon. The narrative of the restoration is emplotted as a
miracle.

Clarendon was a genuinely and deeply pious man. There is in the
final book a sincerely religious fervor which emphasizes the miraculous course that events took. The restoration showed God at work,
not figuratively, but literally. In this sense Clarendon sublimates
himself and other contributing factors to a presentation of God's
providence. God's triumphant vindication of Clarendon's policy
impels the narrative on:

In this wonderful manner, and with this miraculous expedition, did God
put an end in one month...to a rebellion that had raged near twenty
years, and been carried on with all the horrid circumstances of parricide,
murder, and devastation, that fire and the sword, in the hands of the
wickedest men in the world, could be ministers of, almost to the desolation
of two kingdoms, and the exceeding defacing and deforming the third. Yet
did the merciful hand of God in one month bind up all these wounds, and
even make the scars as undiscernible as in respect of their deepness was
possible. (16:247)

The emplotment explains as well the curiously anticlimatic
ending to the *History*. Having finished the passage quoted above,
Clarendon's narrative continues:

And if there wanted more glorious monuments of this deliverance, posterity would know the time of it by the death of the two great favourites of the
two Crowns, cardinal Mazaryne and don Lewis de Haro, who both died
within three or four months, with the wonder, if not the agony, of this
undreamed of prosperity, and as if they had taken it ill that God Almighty

would bring such a work to pass in Europe without their concurrence and against all their machinations.(16:247)

Even for a man as deeply interested in the power of the individual personality as Clarendon was there is still a curious disproportion in ending the *History* on such a note. The ending seems to grow, however, out of the particular emplotment. If the restoration of Charles II was evidence of God's providence, the deaths of the two power brokers of France and Spain, who had done everything they could to obstruct any assistance toward that restoration, was evidence of God's retribution.

Plot structures bring to a series of events not only order, but also meaning. The restoration of Charles II is explained as a miracle and correspondingly the reader brings to the account a set of culturally and mythically determined expectations. White explains the process:

The original strangeness, mystery, or exoticism of the events is dispelled and they take on a familiar aspect, not in their details, but in their functions as elements of a familiar kind of configuration.... They are familiarized, not only because the reader now has more information about the events, but also because he has been shown how the data conform to an icon of a comprehensible finished process, a plot-structure with which he is familiar as a part of his cultural endowment.[8]

Readers might well reject the structure seen or imposed by Clarendon. Certainly anyone who saw the hand of God at work in the overthrow of Charles I's government—Milton, for example—could not possibly have agreed with Clarendon's configuration of the restoration. Nevertheless, the point is that the configuration itself will, for many readers, endow the event with a particular set of meanings. It sanctions, in a sense, the "divine right of kings." The further one goes with this idea, however, the more dangerous those assumptions become.

The plot configuration of any particular episode is independent of the emplotment of the work as a whole. There are other "miraculous" episodes in the *History*, but this is not the structure of the entire *History*. Perhaps because of its size and patchwork composition little attention has been paid to the plot-structure which underlies the work. As we saw in the previous chapter, the analogues for Clarendon's work have traditionally been found among the works of classical historians. It is commonplace to consider Clarendon an English Thucydides or Tacitus, although the analogies are never pursued much farther than a simple assertion. The parallels between the *History* and its classical models are significant and the *History* as a history owes much to its classical precedessors; however, in its final form the *History* owes much as well to the epic tradition.

White argues that the historian emplots "the whole set of stories making up his narrative in one comprehensive or *archetypal* story form."[9] Following Northrop Frye's classification of plot structures, White identifies four different modes of emplotment: romance, tragedy, comedy, and satire. He concedes that there may well be other modes—such as the epic—but that for the historian raised on classical and Christian literature, emplotment must almost inevitably fall into patterns derived from "fiction." "Historical 'stories,'" he continues, "tend to fall into the categories elaborated by Frye precisely because the historian is inclined to resist construction of the complex peripeteias which are the novelist's and dramatist's stock in trade. Precisely because the historian is not (or claims not to be) telling the story 'for its own sake,' he is inclined to emplot his stories in the most conventional forms."[10] Historical narratives thus become "extended metaphors."

Properly understood, histories ought never to be read as unambiguous signs of the events they report, but rather as symbolic structures, extended metaphors, that "liken" the events reported in them to some form with which we have already become familiar in our literary culture.[11]

Whether Clarendon was consciously influenced by specific classical or renaissance epics or by contemporary theorizing about the epic form is not the issue here. Rather, what I am arguing is that in emplotting his narrative, Clarendon seems to have used the epic mode. That mode is, in part, distinguished by a number of conventions and characteristics. These include a hero of significant stature, a setting of significant scope, an action requiring deeds of courage, some supernatural intervention, a style possessing formal grandeur, and an "epic voice" to narrate objectively the great action. There are other incidental features which an epic might show including beginning in medias res and using formal set speeches and epic similes. These are all conventions, not requirements, of the genre, and not every epic would display all of them. Any work of the scope and magnitude of the *History* would possess an epic quality; however, the parallels between the genre or mode and the form of the *History* are striking.

E. M. W. Tillyard was one of the first critics to point to the epic quality of the *History*. The parallel that Tillyard sees is in the shaping of plot and the handling of character:

There is even the chance that when he inserted the great character-sketches in the original portion of the history written in Scilly and Jersey he had an eye to the way Homer conducted the *Iliad*. As Homer began with the origin of the Greeks' trouble in the quarrel of Agamemnon and Achilles, so Clarendon began with the fatal influence of the Duke of Buckingham in getting Parliament dissolved and alienating men's affections from the King. And just as Homer put his catalogues of forces and descriptions of leaders in the pause after the main motivating action had been recounted, so Clarendon introduced his characters of the main actors after he had finished his account of the origins of the rebellion. Not only does Clarendon up to this point construct homerically, he resembles Homer in endowing his characters with much power over events.[12]

Tillyard's observations are concerned with the plot structure of Book I of the *History* and they raise what is the central issue behind the final construction of the *History*. As we saw in chapter 2, Clarendon produced Book I by inserting two long sections taken from his "Life" into the original material written for the "History"—the long digression on the Duke of Buckingham and the character sketches of the chief ministers in 1628 (1:14-146), and an account of the origins and nature of the ecclesiastical dispute which led to the first Scottish war and a series of reflections on the character and actions of Archbishop Laud (1:166-213). On the surface, it appears a cut-and-paste job; Clarendon was simply using whatever material he could from the "Life" and splicing it into the *History*. Such a view of the process of composition implies that there was no controlling purpose. On the other hand, when the composite Book I is seen in the way suggested by Tillyard, an order emerges. The introduction of the digression on the Duke, for example, alters what had been a straightforward chronological progression of the original narrative. The new order moves from the stately invocation back in time to the reign of James I, then forward again to the present. The structural pattern—beginning in medias res—is characteristic of the epic mode. The placement of the character sketches might well have been influenced by epic models.

Other aspects of the emplotment of the *History* reflect the epic as well. Some are obvious, given the action that Clarendon is narrating. The *History* has battles; Clarendon celebrates the courage of the "warriors" involved. In places he stops to "characterize" those of "note" who died. As we will see in chapter 5, those "characters" which follow battlefield deaths in the original "History" are classic rhetorical performances—encomia or celebrations of the virtue and innocence of the dead. The *History* does have supernatural intervention, in both specific episodes and in the resolution of the whole. For example, Charles II's escape from England after the battle of Worcester in 1651 was, Clarendon records, a "miraculous deliverance, in which there might be seen so many visible impressions of the immediate hand of God" (13:84). Similarly, Charles II's restoration was, as we just saw, a deus ex machina resolution to the whole "rebellion." Such ways of seeing events are not fictional contrivances, but Christian epic explanations of what happened.

Character

The function or purpose of a plot, modern literary critics would argue, is to display and reveal character. The type or nature of character will vary with the literary genre. In an autobiography or a lyric poem or a notebook, an author reveals aspects of his own character. In a biography or a history, an author presents characters of actual persons. In fiction, the author reveals the characters of imaginary persons. Whether the characters are real or imaginary is, for one standpoint, irrelevant. What is important is that character must be present in a work of literature. It is character that provides the link between the work and its reader, that establishes the element of universality.

The historian does not have the same latitude in creating character that the creative writer has. Yet, just as the historian sees a particular plot configuration in a series of events, so he sees or interprets the roles, actions, and motivations of individuals in a particular way. The historian of contemporary events has a distinct advantage. He can at least partially know his characters in a way that no historian of past events ever can. But the knowledge of motivation is always partial; interpretation of human behavior is always biased.

Part of the strength of the *History of the Rebellion* lies in its presentation of character. Clarendon prided himself on his knowledge of men. His *History* is full of character sketches of the principal actors in his drama. The historian, he observed, must know the men and the actions of which he writes. The "Genius and Spirit and Soul of an Historian ... is contracted by the Knowledge and Course and Method of Business, and by Conversation and Familiarity in the Inside of Courts, and the most active and eminent Persons in the Government" (*Tracts*, 180). As his contemporary John Evelyn remarked, the characters in the *History* clearly show that Clarendon knew "not only the persons' outsides, but their very interiors."[13] Clarendon did "know" the men about whom he writes; he can, therefore, offer insights that an outsider could never have. Yet, there are distinct limitations to Clarendon's presentation of character.

For one thing, Clarendon consistently reduces the motivations of men, particularly members of the opposition, to self-interest. There were no political or religious principles except those which agreed with his own. The principal motivation of the "ministers of confusion" in the Long Parliament was merely to secure for themselves a political and social position within Charles's court, that, in other words, in the early stages of the struggle they were not only willing, but anxious to be bought off. "I am persuaded," he wrote, "that even then [in 1642], (and I was at that time no stranger to the persons of most that governed, and a diligent observer of their carriage,) they had rather a design of making themselves powerful with the King and great at Court, than of lessening the power of the one or reforming the discipline of the other" (5:30). Such a view of the self-serving motivations of others extends even into Clarendon's own actions after the restoration. He sought, for example, to win the support of some moderate Presbyterians by promising them preferments in the Church. Rewards for individual men would, he felt, prevent the need for any large scale concessions to the whole Presbyterian party.

Character is revealed in literary texts in three ways: through authorial exposition in which we are told about a character, through action by which we make judgments about a character by his actions, and through dialogue or monologue in which a character is revealed either by what he says or by what others say about him. Clarendon's *History* makes very little use of the third way. Rarely do characters speak. To some small extent, characters are revealed in the *History* through action, but the reader is always directed by Clarendon to "see" those actions in a particular way. Overwhelmingly, Clarendon reveals character by authorial exposition. Indeed the very presence of the character sketches in the *History* shapes our response as readers—we are told how to view the individuals and their actions. The "characters" are judgments in which the actor is measured against Clarendon's set of values. The approach, as we will see in chapter 5, is deductive rather than inductive. Clarendon begins the "character" with a decisive judgment in mind; he then selects and arranges details to support that conclusion.

Plot reveals character; character shapes plot. Character, for Clarendon, is a primary causative principle in history. The restoration might have been a miracle, but the rebellion was the result of a series of mistakes and willful actions made by individual men: "the pride of this man, and the popularity of that; the levity of one, and the morosity of another ... the spirit of craft and subtlety in some,

and the rude and unpolished integrity of others" (1:4). In places, for
Clarendon, the man "is" the age. The equation is synecdochial, a
part represents the whole. For example, Clarendon remarks that
character "mirrors" the age. In Book I of the *History*, as he begins
the incredibly long digression about the Duke of Buckingham, he
explains to the reader that the digression is justified or necessary
because "the nature and character and fortune of the duke ... [are]
the best mirror to discern the temper and spirit of that age" (1:94).
The digression which follows—occupying some forty-six pages in
Macray's edition—serves as an explanation for the origins of the
rebellion. His career becomes a history of the period from 1616 to
1628. Read in this way, the rebellion grows out of a series of events
initiated, almost directly and exclusively, by Buckingham. Out of
the failure of the Spanish match (the proposed marriage between
the Prince of Wales and the Spanish Infanta), a union, Clarendon
tells us, encouraged and negotiated by Buckingham, came the war
with Spain. Out of Buckingham's own "particular passion" came
the war with France: a war "without any colour of reason, or so
much as the formality of a declaration from the King ... the declaration which was published was in the duke's own name, who went
admiral and general of the expedition" (1:86). Out of James I's
efforts to protect Buckingham from the wrath of Parliament came
the manipulations and dissolutions of Parliament. Without a Parliament to grant adequate subsidies, James was forced to rely on
supplemental acts of State in order to raise the necessary monies.
Out of those supplemental acts came the rebellion. The argument
from the point of view of causation is ludicrous—even Clarendon
must have known that—but he simply brushes aside any consideration of other factors: "These calamities originally sprung from the
inordinate appetite and passion of this young man, under the too
much easiness of two indulgent masters, and the concurrence of a
thousand other accidents" (1:88).

The "hero" of the *History* is, in a sense, the monarchy itself. The
interval between the execution of Charles I in 1649 and the restoration of Charles II in 1660 is an awkward one in the *History*.
Deprived of a king around whom to "center" the story, Clarendon's
narrative in Books XII through the early part of XVI drifts from

one minor incident to another. The young exiled king never becomes the focal point for the narrative in these sections. No doubt this is so for a number of reasons. There was, for example, no consistent pattern of action. Charles was an outcast, a wanderer, who was forced to drift about Europe. Furthermore, Clarendon always displayed an element of disapproval toward Charles's personal behavior, particularly his involvements with women. Until the restoration became a reality, Charles is treated as prince rather than king.

The perfect embodiment of the monarchy was, for Clarendon, Charles I. When Clarendon began work on the original "History," he wrote to Secretary Nicholas that the king "will not find himself flattered in it, nor irreverently handled" (*Clarendon State Papers*, 2:289). Throughout all three periods of composition, Clarendon's portrayal of Charles I must have been, from Charles's point of view, very nearly irreproachable. The Charles we see is the public man, the king. Clarendon alludes to his personal life, to his affection for his Queen and his children, but we never are given revealing personal moments. This can be most clearly seen by looking at Clarendon's treatment of James I in Book I. Clarendon records at some length the conversations among James, the prince, and the Duke of Buckingham concerning the proposed journey to Spain to expedite the marriage of the prince and the Spanish infanta. James is portrayed as a weak, emotional man who is manipulated by Buckingham into granting his consent. Clarendon's handling of the scene is totally unlike any other moment in the *History* as can be seen in the exchange which supposedly took place between the king and Lord Cottington:

"Cottington, here is Baby Charles and Stenny," (an appellation he always used of and towards the duke,) "who have a great mind to go by post into Spain to fetch home the Infanta, and will have but two more in their company, and have chosen you for one; what think you of the journey?" He often protested that when he heard the King he fell into such a trembling that he could hardly speak. But when the King commanded him to answer him, what he thought of the journey, he replied, that he could not think well of it, and that he believed it would render all that had been

[done] towards the match fruitless.... Upon which the King threw himself upon his bed, and said, "I told you this before," and fell into new passion and lamentation, that he was undone, and should lose Baby Charles. (1:29)

The portrait of Charles is distinctly biased. It is difficult to judge when Clarendon was simply unaware of certain of Charles's plans and actions and when he was construing actions in the most favorable way or intentionally misrepresenting them. When blame is placed, it is placed not upon Charles himself, but upon his advisors. This is particularly true for events prior to the point that Clarendon left Parliament to join the king in 1642. From then on, Clarendon's attitude toward Charles shifts. Sheltered behind the position created for him by Clarendon, Charles is almost beyond reproach—moving from benevolent father, to victim, to martyr. The portrayal of Charles in the material written for the "Life" in 1668 to 1670 is even more laudatory. The Charles that emerges from the middle books of the *History* is very like the Charles of *Eikon Basilike—The Portraiture of His Sacred Majesty in His Solitudes and Sufferings*—the so-called "King's Book" written by Charles and published just prior to his execution. That Charles is "a man of high conscience who would not shirk duty or compromise principle regardless of personal sacrifice." That Charles, contemporary royalists felt, was "nearer the similitude of God then as he is either a man or king."[14] Such a Charles may well have corresponded to the reality. Royalists such as Clarendon at least thought so. Obviously, Independents, such as Milton, did not. But whether this view of Charles is mythic or realistic, it offers a way of seeing and interpreting character.

Narrative Voice

All fiction is, in some sense, a story told by someone. Similarly, one could argue, all narrative history is a story told by someone. Our sense of a narrator varies from work to work, but no matter how objective or omniscient the narration, the shape of the plot and the presentation of character are still authorial fabrications. The fiction that the narrative historian must preserve, however, is that there is no fiction, only fact. What every narrative historian must do is to elevate personal perception into historical truth. One of the ways that effect is achieved is through the narrative voice.

One aspect of narrative voice is point of view, the vantage point from which the author tells the story to the reader. As might be expected given both the length and the composite nature of the *History*, point of view shifts in the narrative. In places such as the scene among James I, the prince, and the duke quoted earlier, the narration is omniscient. More commonly the narration is third-person limited, where Clarendon "objectively" narrates what he knows. But Clarendon is both narrator and actor, and at times, particularly in the account of the Long Parliament, he objectifies himself as "Mr. Hyde" when he describes his role in various Parliamentary debates. Yet in the material which was later transferred from the "Life," Clarendon generally removed such references replacing them with indefinite pronouns or vague expressions. At still other points in the narrative when Clarendon feels the need to defend either the king or himself, he lapses into the first person. In Book VII when he is defending Charles's conduct with respect to the Irish rebels, he remarks: "Some sober men...did upon such assurance believe that the King had done somewhat in that business of Ireland...which, upon as much knowledge as any man can morally have of a negative, I am sure he never did" (7:340).

Since Clarendon is both narrator and actor, since the *History* is an interpretation of what happened rather than a simple chronicle of events, the narrative voice must seem objective; it must seem authoritative. The *History* is biased; it is a royalist interpretation. Even Clarendon would have admitted that. What must come through, however, is not the bias, but the "rightness" of the king's position. This is not *an* interpretation, this is *the* interpretation. Since Clarendon played a large part in many of the actions that he describes, there are inevitably elements of self-justification and self-affirmation in the narrative. At many points Clarendon is not just defending the king, he is also defending himself. His advice, his positions must seem the only rational choices. This is reflected in the narrative at a number of points. In the early books, before Clarendon was an advisor to the king, royalist policy seems governed by whim (and bad advice). But by Books IV and V, the "paper skirmish" books, the king's position suddenly seems to be the only reasonable one. That position, of course, was created by Clarendon and is made rhetorically credible by the narrative voice, and by the inclusion of so many documents which are also examples of Clarendon's rhetoric. We accept the conclusion Clarendon has led us to: "The King had not only to a degree wound himself out of that labyrinth in which four months before they had involved him with their privileges, fears, and jealousies, but had even so well informed the people that they began to question both their logic and their law.... The King's reasons of his denial made very many conclude the unreasonableness of their demands" (5:150).

The tone of the narrative voice varies considerably from section to section. In places, Clarendon seems detached and objective. In others he rises to indignation. He heaps scorn on individuals and on nations. Sometimes, such as the "invocation" to Book IX, Clarendon, realizing that his criticisms of individuals might be interpreted as personal animosity, offers a disclaimer: "I know myself to be very free from any of those passions which naturally transport men with prejudice towards the persons whom they are obliged to mention, and whose actions they are at liberty to censure" (9:3). More typically, however, he does not hesitate or apologize. The Presbyterian clergy were "senseless and wretched... [their] infectious breath corrupted and governed the people" (10:169); the Barebone's Parliament consisted of "inferior persons, of no quality or name, artificers of the meanest trades... a pack of weak senseless fellows" (14:15). At points, as we will see in chapter 5, Clarendon is truly malicious in his remarks about particular individuals. All of this is, of course, simply good rhetorical strategy—and, no doubt, honest indignation on Clarendon's part.

In some sections, especially those from the original "History," Clarendon will adopt the role of advisor. Writing about the king's refusal to agree to the articles of cessation in 1643, he confides to the reader: "I am persuaded, if the King had, upon the receipt of the articles for the cessation, when they were first sent to him, frankly consented to it, it would have proved very much to his advantage" (6:376). Clarendon acts as judge, as in the case of Colonel Fielding who was tried for his surrender of Reading: "I must profess for my part, being no stranger to what was then alleged and proved on either party, I do believe him to have been free from any base compliance with the enemy, or any cowardly declension of what was reasonably to be attempted" (7:43).

The narrative voice is also characterized in part by the figurative language which Clarendon employs. Considering the size of the *History* there is, quantitatively, relatively little. What there is, however, falls into several consistent patterns. Most obviously, as the title of the *History* states, what occurred in England was for Clarendon a "rebellion." In the early books, the "contrivers of the mischief" (4:36) and "ministers of confusion" (4:note to 149) are seen as subverting the royal edifice: they were "removing foundations" (3:36); they sought to "remove the landmarks and to destroy the foundation of the kingdom" (3:208); their actions were "a violence, and removing landmarks, and not a shaking (which might settle again) but dissolving foundations, which must leave the building unsafe for habitation" (4:40); they sought to "subvert the royal building, for supporting whereof they were placed as principal pillars" (4:76).

The rebellion itself is likened to a disease or fire: "Those rough and violent diseases" (5:446), "strange wild-fire" (6:39), the "fatal disease of the whole kingdom" (6:257), "the disease [which] was too violent and catching, and the contagion too universal, to be cured by that remedy" (7:285), "snatching him [Charles I] as a brand out of the fire, and redeeming him even out of the hands of the rebels, more burning and devouring than the most raging fire" (8:57).

Acts of deliverance, moments of victory, and the restoration itself are seen by Clarendon as acts of God. The king's ability to raise troops in 1642 is attributed to "the wonderful providence of God" (6:71); the defeats handed the Irish rebels were "as great instances of God's own detestation of those inhuman rebels, by the signal victories He gave against them" (6:296); the death of the Earl of Essex, before he could give some "check to the rage and fury" that prevailed in London and Parliament is evidence of God's justice: "God would not suffer a man who, out of the pride and vanity of his nature rather than the wickedness of his heart, had been made an instrument of so much mischieve, to have any share in so glorious a work" (10:80). The "deliverance" of Charles II after his escape from Worcester is "the inspiration and conduct of God Almighty, as a manifestation of his power and glory, and for the conviction of that whole nation, which had sinned so grievously" (13:108).

One pervasive pattern which underlies many of the narrative voice's attitudes toward aspects of the rebellion is irony. Clarendon often seems puzzled that the king's cause—a cause which was "right," which embodied the principles of order and established government—fared so poorly on the battlefield. "One side," he observed, "seemed to fight for monarchy with the weapons of confusion, and the other to destroy the King and government with all the principles and regularity of monarchy" (7:276). What fascinated Clarendon—and this becomes a recurrent theme in the later sections of the *History*—was the final irony of the revolutionary situation. Those who were primarily responsible for the destruction of Charles I and the monarchy had been "men of quality." But after the execution of Charles, there was a total change in the sociopolitical hierarchy. Those in power were no longer gentlemen, but commoners—men of no property, position, or manners. After the Self-Denying Ordinance, even the army was no longer led by the nobility, but by men who had risen through the ranks. For Clarendon this truly revolutionary turn was neither explicit nor implicit at the start of the rebellion. None of the king's parliamentary critics would ever have advocated or condoned such a revolution. If Charles II had been delighted by reflections upon such a reversal, he would have had abundant evidence with Scotland, Ireland, and England. Of England, Clarendon writes:

Though the King's heart was even broken with the daily information he received of the ruin and destruction that his faithful and loyal party underwent...yet he could not be equally afflicted to see those who had been the first authors of the public calamity to be now so much sharers in it, that they were no more masters of their estates than they were whom they had first caused to be spoiled, and that themselves were brought and exposed upon those scaffolds which they had caused to be erected for others; that no part of the new government was in any of their hands which had pulled down the old ... and that those lords without whose monstrous assistance the sceptre could never have been wrested out of the hands of the King were now numbered and marshalled with the dregs of the people. (15:3)

Finally, it is the voice of Clarendon that holds the narrative together; it is his voice which breaches the hiatus created by the Interregnum. At a number of places in the narrative Clarendon imposes limits on his story. In the early books these limitations include, for example, events in Scotland and Ireland and accounts of particular military actions and campaigns. After the execution of Charles I, the limitations become infinitely greater, for now the narrative excludes nearly everything happening in England. We are limited to a view of the court in exile with only occasional flashes back to England. The narrative, seen as a "history of the rebellion," is a very partial account of the period. This is normally explained by the circumstances of Clarendon's own life. He was in exile, cut off from any direct knowledge of events in Cromwell's government or even in England itself. Yet that is only part of the answer. Surely another significant factor is that the last half to two-thirds of the *History* was written long after the Restoration. Clarendon knew how things turned out; he knew that the rebellion was finally just a temporary disruption, an interregnum. There was continuity and his narrative voice is what holds it all together. One might add that, ironically, Clarendon himself fell victim to his own fiction. The restoration did not restore an England of the 1640s; the "rebellion" was not just a temporary disruption; it was not to revert to "business as usual." Clarendon's inability to adapt to the changed political climate ultimately resulted in his impeachment and exile.

Despite its size and its patchwork nature, Clarendon's *History of the Rebellion* emerges as a coherent, unified work of art. In transforming a record of historical events into a story, Clarendon, like any narrative historian, utilizes the same literary devices that a writer of fiction would use. Clarendon emplots particular episodes of his story to conform to preconceived plot structures, structures that provide both shape and meaning. The *History* as a whole shows the same process at work. The very shape and nature of Clarendon's *History* provides an interpretation of the events of the period. That interpretation is, in part, reinforced by Clarendon's presentation of character. The actors in the *History* were "real" people, but their actions and motivations are interpreted for us by Clarendon. Correspondingly, they "fit" into the type of story that he is telling. Throughout the *History* it is the voice of Clarendon that converts events into story. It is the voice which gives us a way of making sense of it all, that provides perspectives through point of view, tone, figurative language, and irony. Clarendon's *History* is the first English historical work to become, as well, a work of art.

Chapter Five
The "Character" Sketches

After the Restoration when Clarendon had reached the height of his influence and fortune, he began construction of a sumptuous residence, Clarendon House, in London. John Evelyn, the diarist, visited the house after its completion and described in a letter to Samuel Pepys the many portraits hung on its walls. It was Clarendon's purpose, Evelyn writes, "to furnish all the rooms of state and other apartments with the pictures of the most illustrious of our nation, especially of his lordship's time and acquaintance."[1] Few men have ever taken as much pride in their friendships as he did. In his *Life* he had remarked: "He never took more pleasure in any thing than in frequently mentioning and naming those persons who were then his friends, or of his most familiar conversation, and in remembering their particular virtues and faculties" (*Life*, 1:25). Clarendon's literary counterpart to his collection of paintings is found in the *History of the Rebellion*. Scattered throughout the *History* are character sketches—about 130—of the men who shaped the events of the civil war years, and these sketches have long been regarded as one of the important aspects of the *History*.[2]

The "character" was a popular literary genre in seventeenth-century England. Basically it can be broken down into two categories: the sketch of a specific individual and the sketch of a general type. Those of the first category are generally found in histories and memoirs dating from the period; those of the second are found in "character" collections, anthologies of brief sketches of moral, psychological, social, or occupational types. Both kinds of characters are ultimately derived from classical sources: the first from Greek and Roman histories by writers such as Thucydides, Tacitus, and Plutarch; the second from the "characters" of the Greek writer Theophrastus. Both traditions influenced Clarendon's character sketches.

Classical Influences on the "Character"

It is difficult to assess the impact of any particular classical historian on Clarendon's thought, for few men of the period were as widely read as he. We can establish, though, in some detail the writers to whom Hyde turned when he began work on his "History." In August 1647, about one year after his arrival in Jersey and while he was at work on the first version of the "History," he wrote to a friend: "That you may not think I am idle, I have read over Livy and Tacitus, and almost Tully's [Cicero's] works, and have written ... near 300 large sheets of paper" (*Clarendon State Papers*, 2:375). Among the Clarendon manuscripts which survive are two collections of notes from his readings taken from 1646 to 1673.[3] Here the classical historians are represented by Thucydides, Livy (notes dated 1648), and Plutarch (notes dated 1646). Any extensive analysis of influence must lie outside of the limits of a study such as this; nevertheless, it is possible to touch briefly upon some areas of influence with regard to character.

In *De Oratore* Cicero offers a theory of history writing which is consistent with the aims and methods of Greek and Roman historians. With regard to characters, he remarks: "As for the individual actors, besides an account of their exploits, it [history] demands particulars of the lives and characters of such as are outstanding in renown and dignity."[4] One consistent concern of nearly all of the classical historians was the emphasis upon the individual—what he said or thought, how he acted and why. Causes spring from the actions or inactions of men rather than from social or economic factors. History records the deeds of famous men or the villainy of infamous men for a didactic purpose: to provide the reader with examples of political and moral behavior.

The historians whom Clarendon read consistently reflect this attitude. Thucydides in the opening book of *The History of the Peloponnesian War* points to the value of his work: "Whoever shall wish to have a clear view both of the events which have happened and of those which will some day, in all human probability, happen again in the same or a similar way—for these to adjudge my history profitable will be enough for me."[5] In the

Annals, Tacitus offered a similar view: "This first duty of history—
to ensure that merit shall not lack its record and to hold before the
vicious word and deed the terrors of posterity and infamy."[6] Livy, in
his *Ab Urbe Condita*, remarked: "What chiefly makes the study of
history wholesome and profitable is this, that you behold the
lessons of every kind of experience set forth as on a conspicuous
monument; from these you may choose for yourself and for your
own state what to imitate, from these mark for avoidance what is
shameful in the conception and shameful in the result."[7]

These same values are reflected in Plutarch's *Lives*, a collection
of twenty-three pairs of biographies of Greek and Roman public
figures. Plutarch's heroes are men active in political life and their
actions, in turn, determine the course of history. As Alan Wardman
has observed: "Plutarch's whole approach to character is affected
by his insistence on man's role as a 'politicus': he wants to know
how an individual has acquitted himself while holding office or
submitting to the rule of others."[8] What Clarendon shares with the
classical historians is an emphasis upon the individual as shaper
and determiner of events. With Plutarch he shares as well a
concern for assessing an individual's qualifications or abilities to
fulfill his part in political or military affairs.

The second type of character, the sketch of a general type, also
has classical roots, for the "character" as a literary genre began with
Theophrastus's *Characters*, written about 320 B.C. In a series of
thirty brief (roughly 250 to 300 words) sketches, Theophrastus
defines and then illustrates a particular type of person. Neither
really virtuous or vicious, his characters include such types as the
insincere man, the flatterer, the officious man, the stingy man, the
slanderer. Theophrastus's method is to start with a definition and
then to give examples of actions which are typical of the type. Thus,
the character of the faultfinder begins:

Faultfinding is being unreasonably critical of your portion in life. For
example, a friend sends over a serving of the main dinner course with his
compliments: the faultfinder is the kind who says to the messenger, "You
can go tell your master I said that he didn't want me to have a taste of his
soup and his third-rate wine—that's why he wouldn't give me a dinner
invitation."[9]

Theophrastus's characters surfaced in England when Isaac Casaubon published in 1592 an edition of the Greek text with a Latin translation. The English character, an obvious imitation of the Theophrastan, was born with the publication of John Hall's *Characters of Vertues and Vices* (1608). Hall's intention was clearly didactic. In his introductory remarks, he speaks of characters as "so many speaking pictures, or living images, whereby the ruder multitude might... learn to know virtue and discern what to detest."[10] The 1614 edition catalogues eleven virtuous types (wise man, honest man, faithful man) and fifteen vicious types (busybody, malcontent, flatterer). Hall's methods of development are more complicated, and less vivid, than Theophrastus's. Hall usually starts with a generalization, often involving figurative language or paradox; follows with an examination of motive and representative behavior, phrased in antithetically balanced rhythms; and ends with a rhetorical flourish and often an epigram.

The most prominent example of English character writing came, however, with the publication of the characters of Sir Thomas Overbury and his "friends." These began with a group of twenty-two characters which appeared appended to the second impression (1614) of Overbury's long poem *A Wife.* By 1622 there were eighty-two characters in print—the additional ones written principally by John Webster and Thomas Dekker. No longer are the characters limited to virtues and vices for the Overburian characters reach out to embrace social classes and occupations as well: a country gentleman, a sailor, a tailor, a Puritan, an Inns of Court man, a puny clerk, a virtuous widow, an ordinary widow. The method of development is often that used by Hall; the language is an exaggerated, rhetorical wit. The sketches, as Benjamin Boyce has observed, are "lavishly conceitful,"[11] a prose equivalent to metaphysical poetic wit. The result is that verbal ingenuity often takes precedence over characterization and definition.

The third and last significant collection of English characters was John Earle's *Microcosmography* (1628). In this edition Earle's collection includes fifty-four characters ranging from virtues and vices to social classes and occupations. Generally avoiding the moralistic and satiric methods of the Overburian character, Earle returned to the Theophrastan emphasis upon universal aspects of human character. Earle, as noted earlier, had ties to Clarendon through Lucius Cary, viscount Falkland, at whose home, Great Tew, Earle was a frequent guest. Earle's character is sketched in Clarendon's *Life*. It, interestingly enough, provides another link between the two men for the similarities between Clarendon's characters of Earle and Chillingworth and Earle's "A Downright Scholar" and "A Skeptic in Religion" suggest that Earle might, as Boyce has observed, "on occasion have passed off a portrait of an individual as a Character of a type." [12]

Whether or not Earle might have diverged on a particular character, the intention of the writer of character was to "picture" a type and to isolate its moral or psychological or social characteristics. The influence of the character tradition on Clarendon's portraiture was subtle rather than overt. Clarendon's characters were, after all, portraits of real men rather than of types. But the influence of character writing in the seventeenth century did focus attention especially on the moral and psychological aspects of human behavior. Human nature was analyzed and classified. It was this aspect of the tradition that perhaps most clearly influenced Clarendon.

Clarendon, the "Character," and Historical Causation

Clarendon did not introduce character sketches into the *History* simply because he was conforming either to classical models or to the contemporary vogue for character studies. Their presence is also a reflection of both his ideas of historical causation and of the "end" or purpose of a history.

We have already examined Clarendon's views on causation at some length so an example or two should suffice here. Clarendon has often been criticized for, as one critic observed, ignoring the "general causes" of the rebellion and "over estimat[ing] the influence of individuals and the importance of personal causes." [13] It is fair to say that from 1646 until he finished the *History* in 1671 he never changed his attitude: the rebellion occurred not because of irresistible social, economic, or religious issues, but because of the failures, mistakes, and intentional actions of individual men whether those men were the king's advisors or military officers, or the "contrivers of the mischief" (4:36) in Parliament. In his preface to the original "History" written in 1645, Hyde had announced his intention to focus upon the "atoms" which contributed to this "mass of confusion"—specifically, "the pride of this man, and the popularity of that; the levity of one, and the morosity of another... the spirit of craft and subtlety in some, and the rude and unpolished integrity of others" (1:4). Hyde seems always to have limitless faith in the power of personality to change events. In the incredibly long digression in Book I about the Duke of Buckingham and his influence over government policy, Hyde concludes, for example, that if he had had "one faithful friend" who would have "frankly" advised him, Buckingham would have "committed as few faults, and done as transcendent worthy actions, as any man" of the age (1:70, 71). Throughout the *History* Clarendon pauses to comment on what he feels were the personal motivations behind particular actions. In a passage written in 1671, Clarendon reflects on the "weakness and folly" of the royalists and the "malice and wickedness" of the Parliamentarian opposition. The "lamentable effects" of that year (1645), he continues, "proceeded only from the folly and the frowardness, from the weakness and the wilfulness, the pride and the passion, of particular persons" (9:2).

If particular events, even events as large as the civil war itself, are basically determined by actions and decisions made by individuals, then history should record personalities. In a letter dated 8 January 1647, Clarendon wrote: "I take it to be no less the true end of history, to derive the eminency and virtue of those persons, who lived and acted in those times of which he writes, faithfully to posterity, than the counsels which were taken, or the actions which were done" (*Clarendon State Papers*, 2:328). Elsewhere he wrote: "Celebrating the memory of eminent and extraordinary persons, and transmitting their great virtues for the imitation of posterity [is] one of the principal ends and duties of history" (7:217). As the character sketches in the *History* demonstrate, virtue is not the only quality to be preserved in history, for those guilty of rebellion, or disloyalty, or even weakness should be "charged with their own evil actions" (9:2).

The corollary to these two premises—that political history is shaped and determined by individuals and that the "end" of history is to memorialize good and evil men—is that the historian of contemporary events must be a man of active experience. He must know the men and actions of which he writes. The "Genius and Spirit and Soul of an Historian . . . is contracted by the Knowledge and Course and Method of Business, and by Conversation and Familiarity in the Inside of Courts, and the most active and eminent Persons in the Government" (*Tracts*, 180). It was this knowledge and experience that contributed immeasurably to the success of Clarendon's characters. As his contemporary John Evelyn remarked, the characters clearly show that Clarendon knew "not only the persons' outsides, but their very interiors."[14]

The Development of the Clarendon Character

In its final form the *History of the Rebellion* contains about 130 character sketches. The number is approximate because it is sometimes difficult to decide when a section qualifies as a character and when it does not. Basically the Clarendon character can be defined as a relatively brief verbal portrait of a person's essential qualities. It is a degression from the narrative; it is static in the sense that character values are assessed by judgment rather than revealed through action or dialogue. Typically Clarendon focuses upon a person's family, his education or experience, his moral values, his psychological traits, or his social behavior. The characters are judgments of the actors in the *History*, judgments that are generally impartial and certainly always decisively final. They vary in length from several sentences to approximately twelve pages. Most, however, run about one to two paragraphs in length. The characters were not equally distributed throughout the three periods of composition: 20 were written for the original "History" during the years 1646 to 1648; 103 were written for the "Life" during the years 1668 to 1670; and a final 7 were added when the two manuscripts were worked together in 1671 to 1672 to make the final *History*. Since both the distribution and the nature of the characters are related to when they were written, we will begin by looking at some differences between the early and the late characters.

That there were so few characters in the original "History" is not surprising when we remember how Hyde perceived of that work. It was to be an instructive guide to past mistakes, and, by implication, to future political conduct. To stress this pragmatic, "state paper" aspect of the original "History" does not mean that Hyde was oblivious to the literary aspects of his work. Even in 1646 Hyde was consciously imitating, in an indirect way, classical models. What he did not do, however, was to use the character to exemplify or explain the age in the same way that he did in the "Life."

There is no consistent pattern of placement for the character sketches in the original "History." Despite Hyde's emphasis upon the errors and inadequacies of the king's advisors, there are only two instances where he sketches a character. In the first, after he has discussed the various means by which Charles I had raised money—illegal means for Hyde—and then had gotten judges to uphold the legality of those means, Hyde pauses for two character sketches—those of William Noy, the Attorney General, and Lord Finch, then Lord Keeper of the Great Seal(1:157, 158). They were responsible for the mischief; they profaned the profession of law by making it subservient to the government's desires. In the second, Hyde sketches Strafford, Lord Cottington, and Hamilton (2:101, 102, 103), the principal members of the king's Committee of State. Where the characters of Noy and Finch had been essentially limited to their legal inadequacies, these are barely characters at all—a sentence or two of judgment trailing off into an assessment of the attitudes that people had toward each.

Only once does Hyde relate character to the age. As an example of the "unruly and mutinous spirit" of London, "the sink of all the ill humour of the kingdom" (3:57), he offers brief portraits of William Prynne, John Bastwick, and Henry Burton, the three dissidents previously censured for their criticisms of the government of church and state. The characters, however, are merely excuses for invective. Prynne's writings are "absurd, petulant, and supercilious" (3:59); Bastwick was a "half-witted, crack-brained fellow" (3:60); and Burton was endued "with malice and boldness, instead of learning and any tolerable parts" (3:61).

The character does not really develop in the original "History" until Hyde uses it to commemorate the dead. Part of the function of history was, Hyde had written, "to transmit the virtue of excellent persons to posterity." He continued, "I am careful to do justice to every man who hath fallen in the quarrel, on which side soever" (*Clarendon State Papers*, 2:386). Two of the death sketches—the first and the last—were not connected with battlefield injuries and they demonstrate nicely how Hyde manipulated the character to achieve a rhetorical end. The first character is given to Strafford (3:204-5) after his execution. Unlike the earlier mention of him (2:101), this is a fully developed character which balances his extraordinary abilities against his prideful arrogance. The controlling impression which emerges is of a man whose destruction is insured by his tragic flaw—pride. The character of Parliamentary leader John Pym (7:409-13) on the other hand concentrates almost exclusively on recording his actions in Parliament. It is a clever and probably conscious choice, for although Hyde expresses admiration for his skill as a leader, he is also able to question the integrity of his actions. He suggests first that Pym could have been bought off by the offer of a place in Charles's government, that he used unscrupulous tricks in the prosecution of Strafford, and that he took bribes.

The ten remaining characters in the original "History" all occur after battlefield deaths. They vary greatly in length and detail from short, simple accounts of how an individual died to the longest character sketch in the entire *History*—that of Lucius Cary, Viscount Falkland (7:217-34). Despite his claim to treat both sides, Hyde sketches nine royalists but only one parliamentarian. These sketches are rarely balanced; they are, instead, encomia—celebrations of the virtue and innocence of the dead. Sidney Godolphin, who fell at Chagford, engaged himself "out of the pure indignation of his soul and conscience" against the "wickedness" of Commons (6:251). The earl of Northampton, killed at Hopton Heath, was the perfect warrior: "no man more punctual upon command, no man more diligent and viligant in duty. All distresses he bore like a common man" (6:283). Of Sir Nicholas Slanning and Colonel John Trevannion who died at Bristol, Hyde writes: "whose memories can never be enough celebrated ... led by no impulsion but of conscience" (7:132). Lord Grandison, also killed at Bristol, was "of that rare piety and devotion that the court or camp could not shew a more faultless person, or to whose example young men might more reasonably conform themselves" (7:133).

The only long characters of this group are those of John Hampden, the parliamentarian, and Lucius Cary. The character of Hampden is impartial, indeed even favorable. In both Hyde ranges widely—details from their lives, assessments of the social, psychological, and moral behavior. Both show as well the influence of classical models. Hyde concludes the character of Hampden with an epigram derived from Cicero's oration on Catiline: "He had a head to contrive, and a tongue to persuade, and a hand to execute, any mischieve" (7:84).[15] The long character of Falkland, on the other hand, recalls Tacitus's *Life of Agricola,* a parallel Hyde himself points out at several places in the character. In terms of length, detail, and tone, the character of Falkland is a complete anomaly when judged against the other characters in the original "History." Hyde was aware of this for he wrote to John Earle on 14 December 1647: "It may be I have insisted longer upon the argument [the character] than may be agreeable to the rules to be observed in such a work; though it be not much longer than Livy is in recollecting the virtues of one of the Scipio's after his death." If it is "unproportionable for the place," he continues, perhaps it would be best to "make it a piece by itself, and inlarge it into the whole size of his life; and that way it would be sooner communicated to the world. And you know Tacitus published the Life of Julius Agricola, before either of his annals or his history" (*Clarendon State Papers,* 2:386).

With one or two exceptions the characters in the original "History" are not as developed as those which date from the later periods of composition, nor are they as plentiful. Hyde seems principally to have used the character as a way of eulogizing the dead. What he does not do is to survey the personalities involved in the struggle. Characters do not, in that sense, reveal the age. In part, this is probably a reflection of Hyde's original intention in the "History." It is possible as well that it might have seemed presumptuous for Hyde in 1648, still essentially a civil servant to Charles I, to write the type of character that he could write in 1668. By then, Hyde was Viscount Cornbury and Earl of Clarendon; he had twenty years of experience; he had been one of the most powerful men in England. He could judge now in a way that would not have been possible before.

The overwhelming number of characters in the *History*—103 of the 130 total—were originally written for the "Life" during the years 1668 to 1670 and were then transferred into the final *History*. The "Life" was not an autobiography in the sense that we might expect. Rather, it was a record of Clarendon's role in the course of events. It does not seem surprising that Clarendon, looking back over the events of his life and the people he had known, would have included character sketches. Some interesting differences between the early characters and these late ones are immediately obvious.

By this point, for Clarendon the age itself is explained by the personalities of those in power, as if to "know" the men explains what happened. Causes are personal. In Book I, for example, before the long digression about the Duke of Buckingham, Clarendon explains: "It will give much light to that which follows if we take a view of the state of the Court and of the Council at that time, by which, as in a mirror, we may best see the face of that time, and the affections and temper of the people in general" (1:13). The majority of these later characters occur in groups as Clarendon digresses from his narrative to survey the actors: the fourteen chief ministers under Charles I in 1628; the nine "great contrivers and designers" in Parliament; the fourteen Privy Councillors who attended the king; the nine who stayed behind in London; the four military advisors; the thirteen ambassadors to and members of the Spanish court. Even among the smaller groupings or the scattered isolated characters, the choice is always the influential individual—the advisor, the military leader. Despite the large number of characters, only fourteen follow battlefield deaths and none of these is an encomium as those in the original "History" had been.

Among the groupings there is occasionally an even more subtle rationale for their presence and their selectivity of detail. The first large group of characters—eleven in all—come in Book I when Clarendon digresses from the narrative of events to characterize the chief ministers under Charles I in 1628. Clarendon specifically proposes to treat "how equal their faculties and qualifications were for those high transactions" (1:95). Of all the groups of sketches in the *History* these are the longest and the nastiest. Composed in 1668–69, they date from immediately after Clarendon's fall from power.[16] As soon as he settled in France, Clarendon had begun work on his "A Discourse, by Way of Vindication of my self from the Charge of High-Treason" and simultaneously, on his "Life." It is obvious that in this group of characters, more so than any of the others, Clarendon is consciously judging each man in light of the charges of treason which had just been leveled at him. These characters are, in this sense, vindications of Clarendon's own behavior and reflections upon the instability of any position of power.

The principal failing of many of these ministers is greed. Nine of the seventeen charges against Clarendon involved bribery and other financial irregularities. Of Sir Richard Weston, Lord High Treasurer, Clarendon, for example, remarks: "No man had greater ambition to make his family great, or stronger designs to leave a great fortune to it" (1:108). The Earl of Manchester, Lord Privy Seal, was "too solicitous to advance [his fortunes] by all the ways which offered themselves" (1:117); the Earl of Arundel "got all he could, and by all the ways he could" (1:119); the Earl of Carlisle was "a man of the greatest expense in his own person of any in the age" (1:135); Sir John Cook, Secretary of State, was addicted to his "appetite" for money (1:142). At the end of the character section, Clarendon remarks of the group of ministers as a whole: "Much the greater part of them would be wholly intent upon their own accommodations in their fortunes . . . and in their ease and plea-sure" (1:146).

Clarendon reflects as well upon the precariousness of such positions of power. Sir Thomas Coventry, Lord Keeper of the Seal, died in office. Clarendon commends his "strength and skill (as he was an excellent wrestler)" which preserved him so long in an office "so slippery" that "no man had died in it before for near . . . forty years" (1:96). For Sir Richard Weston, Clarendon changes the analogy: "He did swim in those troubled and boisterous waters . . . with a good grace, when very many who were about him were drowned, or forced on shore with shrewd hurts and bruises" (1:104).

A somewhat similar, but less aggressively defensive, rationale prefaces the very large group of characters of the Privy Councillors. In the "Life" Clarendon had reached the point when he himself was first sworn a Privy Councillor. He digresses to "set down the state of the Court and the state of the kingdom" by giving a series of characters, so that, he continues defensively, "it will easily appear how little motive any man could have from interest or ambition, who was not carried by the impulsion of conscience and considera-tion of duty, to engage himself in the quarrel on the King's side" (6:382).

The farther Clarendon wrote in his "Life" and the more distant the traumatic events of his own recent past became, the less the characters seem tied to self-justification. Over half of the characters from the "Life" occur in the first six books of the *History*. The remaining characters are, with a single exception, scattered fairly evenly through the last ten books. The only exception is the group of thirteen characters which comes during the embassy of Claren-don and Cottington to Spain. Clarendon's justification for sketch-ing these characters is slight indeed—"there was no action or counsel [more important] to be mentioned at present, and this being the first and only embassy in which his majesty's person was represented until his blessed return into England" (12:92).

The Clarendon Character

The typical Clarendon character as it appears in the *History of the Rebellion* exhibits some distinctive characteristics. It is, for the most part, fair. Virtues where they exist are commended; vices are exposed. The most fully developed of the characters explore both aspects of the individual. He sees, for example, the weaknesses of

Charles I and the strengths of that "brave bad man" (15:156), Oliver Cromwell. The voice of the narrator, with its formal, magisterial tone, helps foster the illusion of the finality and accuracy of the judgments Clarendon passes. The reader is left feeling that this "is" the person rather than merely Clarendon's view. Clarendon does not always, however, play fair. In the later characters especially, Clarendon's criticisms can be malicious and condescending. In what is the nastiest of the sketches—the Earl of Arundel— Clarendon writes that although he had a rare collection of medals, he was "only able to buy them, never to understand them; and as to all parts of learning he was most illiterate" (1:119). While remarking on the Earl of Pembroke's lascivious practices, Clarendon notes: "He paid much too dear for his wife's fortune by taking her person into the bargain" (1:123). The Earl of Montgomery had no qualifications for his position other than "to understand horses and dogs very well" (1:128). Archbishop Abbot was "totally ignorant of the true constitution of the Church of England, and the state and interest of the clergy" (1:185).

Clarendon never, however, ridicules or even mentions physical features. At best he is general, as in he was "handsome." This was not always so in the character writing tradition. For example, Bishop Burnet in his *History of His Own Times* described the Earl of Lauderdale: "He made a very ill appearance: He was very big: His hair red, hanging oddly about him: His tongue was too big for his mouth, which made him bedew all that he talked to." [17] What interested Clarendon was not the physical characteristics, for these were after all irrelevant externals which did not reveal the personality.

Clarendon does note family, especially if "ancient," "noble," and distinguished; education; travel or experience in government or the military. He singles out for praise a number of social qualities (manners, courtesy, civility, bearing, friendliness), intellectual capacities (wit, cleverness, eloquence, understanding), virtues (humility, industry, generosity, honesty, courage). He admires above all the person who has the ability to manage, and even manipulate, others. He constantly praises the person of "great parts"; he is fond of the adjective "very" to qualify any virtue or vice. The typical Clarendon character blends facts and judgments, balances strengths and weaknesses. For example, the character of the Earl of Leicester begins:

[He] was a man of great parts, very conversant in books, and much addicted to the mathematics; and though he had been a soldier, and commanded a regiment in the service of the States of the United Provinces, and was afterwards employed in several embassies, as in Denmark and in France, was in truth rather a speculative than a practical man, and expected a greater certitude in the consultation of business than the business of this world is capable of: which temper proved very inconvenient to him through the course of his life. (6:387)

Clarendon records and condemns vices (greed, pride, vanity, lust), the lack of essential social graces (moroseness, rudeness), the lack of intelligence or good judgment, the lack of control (the indulgence in women, drink or food, extravagance, irresolution, or unbridled ambition). He condemns above all the person who puts self above loyalty, fidelity, integrity, and conscience—and needless to say those qualities were, for Clarendon, found principally among the royalists. When Clarendon condemns, he does so swiftly and decisively as in the case of Sir John Hotham: "Hotham was, by his nature and education, a rough and a rude man; of great covetousness, of great pride, and great ambition; without any bowels of good nature, or the least sense or touch of generosity" (5:434).

The very fact that the Clarendon character is a judgment in which a person is measured against a consistent and explicit set of values means that the character has a controlling purpose or center. He begins writing a character with a decisive judgment in mind; he then selects and arranges details to support that conclusion. This does not mean, however, that the characters are "flat," or that they portray "types" rather than individuals. Nor does this imply that there is a consistent order of detail or pattern of development followed in every character. With the exception of the battlefield encomia and some of the brief characters, the typical Clarendon character reveals the mixture of motives, the strengths and weaknesses, the idiosyncrasies which characterize human nature.

And finally, it is for this reason that the characters contribute so significantly to the success of the *History of the Rebellion*. Writing as he was about his contemporaries, men whom he knew, Clarendon conveys to the reader a sense of the individuals involved in a way that no modern historian could possibly achieve. Clarendon's judgments are ultimately personal; he does not have the objectivity that time and distance can sometimes bring. His judgments are probably biased; he does probably over-estimate the significance of particular individuals. But what sustains the *History* as a narrative work is Clarendon's vision of men and events. Through his characters he allows us, as readers, to experience an immediacy and an illusion of reality.

Chapter Six

Clarendon's Reply to Hobbes's *Leviathan*

Backgrounds

The period from 1600 to 1660 was a time of enormous political upheaval in England. When James I ascended the throne in 1603, the position and future of the monarchy seemed unassailable despite Parliament's increasing challenge to the limits and nature of the king's authority. In a speech to Parliament in 1610, James asserted: "The state of monarchy is the supremest thing upon earth; for kings are not only God's lieutenants upon earth, and sit upon God's throne, but even by God himself they are called gods."[1] Less than forty years later, James's son Charles I, God's vice-regent on earth, was tried by a court composed of his own subjects, found guilty as a "tyrant, traitor, murderer, and public enemy," and executed. The Interregnum, which followed, saw a variety of political theories and experiments and the eventual restoration of the monarchy in 1660, but a monarchy vastly changed in power and position.

Understandably, the turmoil of the six decades produced some of the finest statements of political philosophy in England's history. Democratic, radical, and royalist theorists debated the fate and form of the government in England in both abstract and pragmatic terms. Of all of the theoretical works which emerged from the period, none occupies a place equal to that of Thomas Hobbes's *Leviathan*. In that Hobbes's ideas were essentially outside the mainstream of seventeeth-century political thought, he provoked a broad range of critics. One of these was Clarendon who in 1676 published *A Brief View and Survey of the Dangerous and pernicious Errors to Church and State, in Mr. Hobbes's Book, Entitled LEVIATHAN.* Clarendon's reply is an important document in terms of seventeenth-century political thought for two closely related reasons. First, Clarendon's position as propagandist and advisor to Charles I and then as Charles II's "most trusted advisor" and "[virtual] head of the [restored] government,"[2] gave him a unique vantage point as a contemporary critic of Hobbes's theories. As John Bowle has observed: "In general, great ministers of State are too busy making history to theorize about politics, and if they record their opinions tend to write memoirs or narrative."[3] Second, Clarendon's reply is pragmatic; he seeks to expose the fundamental political errors contained in *Leviathan.* Political theory must, after all, be judged as well in terms of political reality. Perhaps more than any other man in restoration England, Clarendon was qualified to make such a critique.

Such political thought, both theoretic and pragmatic, can only be understood within the context of political theory and practice in England during the sixteenth and seventeenth centuries. Before examining *Leviathan* and Clarendon's *A Brief View,* it is essential to sketch briefly the basic tenets of political thought in sixteenth-century England, the impact that Machiavelli made on that thought, and the developments brought about by a sharply changing political reality.

Living as we do in an age in which politics is labeled and studied as a social science, it is difficult to imagine the extent to which Englishmen in the sixteenth century lacked any similar concept of politics and political theory as a self-contained activity. For them, politics was linked to religion. Society, the body politic, was divinely ordained and the ruler—whether elected or hereditary—was God's representative on earth. There was essentially no "art" of politics. If it was practiced, as of course it was, it was not written about. Erasmus's popular treatise on political theory was entitled *The Education of a Christian Prince* (1516). Training that a would-be prince needs does not consist of practical advice, but rather an education in his responsibilities as a Christian, for the ruler is "a living likeness of God." Erasmus constantly returns to the analogy: "God placed a beautiful likeness of Himself in the heavens—the sun. Among mortal men he set up a tangible and living image of himself—the king."[4] Disobedience to the ruler was disobedience to God, unless it could be shown that the ruler himself was acting contrary to God's will.

Social and political order were thus seen as reflections of the cosmic order—the "Great Chain of Being." To disrupt that order through disobedience or rebellion was to embrace chaos. The Homily on Obedience (1547), a government established sermon read in the churches, stressed:

For where there is no ryght ordre, there reigneth all abuse, carnal libertie, enormitie, synne, and Babilonical confusyon. Take away kinges, princes, rulers, magistrates, judges, and such estates of god's order, no man shall ryde or go by the hyghway unrobbed, no man shall slepe in his owne house or bed unkylled, no man shal kepe his wyfe, children and possessions in quietnes: all thinges shalbe common, and there must nedes folowe all myschief and utter destruction both of soules, bodies, goodes and commonwealthes.[5]

Such a view of a ruler's position and authority did not imply, however, an endorsement of absolutism. The ruler was limited by two concepts. Although he was God's image or lieutenant in this life, he was responsible to God and He would punish the tyrant, if not in this life, then in the life to come. The *Mirror for Magistrates* (1559), a collection of verse stories about evil rulers and subjects with moralizing commentary in prose, preached obedience to the civil authority with the reassurance that God's justice would ultimately prevail. Furthermore, in England, the monarch was also bound to obey the fundamental laws and customs of the land. A system of common law, regarded by contemporary theorists as immemorial, coexisted with the monarchy. Under this "ancient constitution" the king enjoyed certain prerogatives; but, similarly, his subjects had certain rights. This concept of a "constitution" was intended to prevent the monarch from unilaterally altering or abolishing his subjects' rights and privileges. The law precedes the existence of a monarchy. The issue is clearly stated by J. G. A. Pocock: "If the constitutionalists could show that the laws were as old as, or older than, the kings, they might go on to assert a contractual or elective basis for kingship; but if the laws had come into being at a time when there was already a king, then nothing but the king's authority could have sanctioned them or made them law, and the king might assert a sovereign right to revoke what his predecessors had granted."[6]

The sixteenth century in England was marked by theological controversy and a growing spirit of nationalism. Henry VIII divorced England from the influence and power of the Pope and the Church; Elizabeth presided with both tact and firm control over a nation emerging as an international power. But the seeds for political change were being sown. The old feudal and ecclesiastical principles which were the foundation of Tudor political power no longer held the same force. Political power was passing, for example, from the aristocracy to an emerging middle class. Despite these changes, though, when the seventeenth century began, political theory in England still basically reflected the tenets of the "Elizabethan world picture" outlined above.And, as J. P. Kenyon has observed, that theory was "simple, patriarchal and authoritative, virtually untouched in terms of practical politics by continental writers."[7] That view of politics did not, of course, prevail for long.

To trace the evolution of political theory in England during the sixteenth and seventeenth centuries would require far more space than is available here. Furthermore, to single out individual theories or even a group of theorists would be perhaps to overestimate their significance in terms of the shifting political realities during those years. The civil war in England was, obviously, the result of a number of factors—factors which were for the most part pragmatic, social, economic, and religious in nature rather than philosophic. Still, attitudes toward the basis and nature of government and sovereignty changed so sharply during the 1600s that it is important to note how completely the old Elizabethan view of politics as a handmaiden to theology was replaced by a view of politics as a purely secular act. That change is nowhere as evident as it is in the work of Machiavelli.

Machiavelli and Secular Politics

It is fairly safe to say that the concept of politics in Western thought was revolutionized by Machiavelli—that as one historian has observed, he in fact "invented politics."[8] What is meant is that Machiavelli did more than any other figure to divorce politics from theology, to see it as a self-contained, secular activity. In both *The Prince* and the *Discourses,* Machiavelli replaces the essentially medieval, theological view of society and its relationship to God with an analysis of what the prince must do in order to acquire and then maintain his power. As he wrote in *The Prince*: "Since I intend to write something useful to an understanding reader, it seemed better to go after the real truth of the matter than to repeat what people have imagined."[9] The real view of things is that politics has always been a dirty business. Ernst Cassirer has observed: "No one had ever doubted that political *life,* as matters stand, is full of crimes, treacheries, and felonies. But no thinker before Machiavelli had undertaken to teach the *art* of these crimes."[10] Machiavelli, in short, makes no moral judgments about the activities of the Prince; he is not God's representative on earth; he is not to judge by what is good or evil but by what is expedient and effective. "Any man who tries to be good all the time," Machiavelli writes, "is bound to come to ruin among the great number who are not good. Hence a prince who wants to keep his post must learn how not to be good."[11] The advice that Machiavelli offers his prince includes such lessons as: that when a prince takes over a new country, he should wipe out the family of the previous ruler; that a prince should have no other thought or study than the rules and disciplines of war; that it is better to be feared than loved; that subjects are quicker to forget the death of a father than the loss of a patrimony. As far as religion itself goes, Machiavelli regards it as a useful instrument for controlling subjects: an "instrument necessary above all others for the maintenance of a civilised state."[12]

What Machiavelli introduced into political theory was the concept of political realism. His impact on Tudor and even early Stuart political thought was not particularly significant. At a time when the sovereign's right was de jure, when there was divine right, a strong state religion, and an established order in society, Machiavelli seemed far less relevant than he did in the 1640s after the hereditary monarch had been executed, the official church dismantled, and the sovereign power had become de facto. After the publication of Edward Dacres's translations of the *Discourses* (1636) and *The Prince* (1640), Machiavelli's work reached a much wider English audience. But the extent of Machiavelli's influence on English political thought is not the issue here. Rather, what is important is that with the changing political structure in England, Machiavelli's secular and realistic approach to politics came to have an increasing relevance to the English political scene. Even Clarendon, as noted in chapter 4, was attracted to the shrewd and even ruthless advice which Machiavelli offered to a ruler. In a series of notes which Clarendon made in a commonplace book in 1646-47 while reading Dacres's translation of the *Discourses*, he wrote: "If all History were written by as wise men as Machiavell, and the true grounds and originalls of all difficulties to the State observed, and then remedyed, surely there needs little more wisdom for government, than a dispassionate and sober perusall of those Storyes."[13]

Before turning to an examination of Hobbes's *Leviathan* and Clarendon's *A Brief View,* it remains only to examine briefly the changing political reality in England from the coronation of James I in 1603 until the execution of Charles I in 1642.

The Political Reality: 1603-1642

James I saw the monarchy as a divinely ordained institution. He propounded the theory of the "divine right of kings." The idea did not originate with James, but he was in many ways its most eloquent spokesman. The theory, reduced to its simplest terms, involved the following assertions: monarchy is a divinely ordained institution; hereditary right is indefeasible; kings are accountable to God alone and their power is subject to no legal limitation; and

nonresistance and passive obedience on the part of subjects are
enjoined by God.[14] Nowhere is the theory more clearly stated than
in James's treatise *The Trew Law of Free Monarchies: Or the
Reciprock and Mutuall Dutie Betwixt a Free King and his Naturall
Subjects* (1598). James had argued that God alone could make a
king and that the people must obey their king; they could only resist
his authority by appeals to God. Since kings preceded law, they
were makers of law and hence not bound by it. The king, although
he is both above the people and the law, is responsible to God and
the just and good king acts as a loving father toward his subjects.
Evil or unjust kings exist; sometimes they are sent by God as a
punishment for a people, but it is unlawful and sinful for the people
to rebel against such a king. They are to be patient and pray that
God will remove him.

In an age which "demanded religious sanctions for temporal
things," it was no wonder that James found the theory appealing.
As his biographer observed: "James must of necessity claim the
support of heaven if he hoped to combat the pretensions of the
Kirk, the doctrines of Rome, and the arrogance of the nobles. He
must have a religious sanction for his demand that all classes obey
and reverence their King."[15] Support for James's theories came
from Anglican clergy and from friends of the crown—never from
Parliament. One of his most eloquent supporters was Francis
Bacon whose statements on political theory are not contained
within a single work but rather are scattered throughout a number
of his works. Basically, he argued that a sovereign had an almost
unlimited prerogative. Parliament should regularly be consulted,
but it should neither limit the sovereign's authority nor hold him
accountable for his every act. The significance of Bacon's views do
not rest in either their novelty nor their profundity. Instead, they
served to encourage James in his absolutist theories and, in turn, to
widen the gap between the king and Parliament.

Despite James's rhetoric and Bacon's encouragement, in actual
practice James was careful to move within the limits established by
English law and custom. James himself explained the seeming
contradiction between his theory and his practice in a speech to
Parliament on 21 March 1610, when he contrasted the "state of

kings in their first original" whose "wills...served for law" with the "state of settled kings and monarchies" who are bound to observe "the fundamental laws of the kingdom."[16] As a "settled" king, James was careful to respect the common law and the privileges and authority of Parliament.

Charles I did not seem to share his father's interest in political theory. His most extensive political statements appeared during the "paper skirmishes" he waged with Parliament in 1642 and even then his positions and arguments belonged to his advisors, including Clarendon, rather than to Charles himself. It was during Charles's reign, however, that the fundamental political assumptions upon which the very concept of the English monarchy rested were, at least temporarily, overthrown.

Whatever causes one advances for the civil war which confronted Charles I, there is at least no doubt that in the 1640s the control of the government and of the country—sovereignty— passed from the king to Parliament. The challenge to the king's authority became explicit with Parliament's demand that Charles agree to their Nineteen Propositions in June 1642. Had Charles consented, Parliament would have essentially become head of state. Charles, however, refused and in reply published his Answer to the Nineteen Propositions, the most significant political statement he ever made. The Answer was drafted by Lucius Cary, Viscount Falkland, then secretary of state, and Sir John Culpepper, then chancellor of the exchequer. In it, Charles evoked the theory of "mixed monarchy." The theory, which existed in English political thought for some time, held that England's government consisted of a blend of monarchy (king), aristocracy (House of Lords), and democracy (House of Commons). Government by each "estate" had its own "conveniences" and "inconveniences." What was important was the mixture, the checks and balances that the estates had on one another. "As long as the balance hangs even between the three estates," Charles argued, England enjoyed the virtues of each without the abuses of any one.[17]

Clarendon, however, had disagreed with Falkland and Culpepper over the definition of the three estates. He clung to the more conservative and traditional position. Instead of king, Lords, and Commons, Clarendon argued that the estates consisted of the lords spiritual, the lords temporal, and the commons. The king was "head and sovereign of the whole."[18] Reducing the king to one of three placed a genuine limitation on his sovereignty. Clarendon's objection, which surfaces again in his reply to *Leviathan*, went unheeded and Falkland and Culpepper's definition replaced, for most men, the more traditional view.

There is no doubt that Charles was forced to embrace the mixed monarchy theory by the rapidly deteriorating political situation. His long period of personal rule, during which he did not summon a Parliament, and his various abuses of his authority are clear evidence that until 1642 Charles might well have defined the monarchy in more absolutist terms. Still, the theory quickly became the prevailing view of the English constitution in the mid-seventeenth century, so much so that, Corinne C. Weston has observed, it assumed for many "the sanctity of fundamental law."[19]

Despite its sanctity what eventually happened was that a single estate—the "purged" and hence not even representative House of Commons—legislated the other two estates out of existence. On 4 January 1649 the House of Commons declared itself to have "the supreme power in this nation," and on 6 February 1649, only seven days after the execution of Charles I, the Commons resolved to abolish the House of Lords. The next day, it did the same for the monarchy. The various theoretical and practical attempts to establish a commonwealth or a republic are too complicated to be discussed here and in view of a restored mixed monarchy in 1660 are irrelevant to our concern. There is certainly some validity in arguing, though, that the Restoration in part came about because England was unable to establish an acceptable alternative to the "mixed" monarchy.

The question of the nature and scope of sovereignty is, however, crucial to the theories of Hobbes as expressed in *Leviathan* and *Behemoth* and of Clarendon in *A Brief View*. In *Leviathan*, as we will see, Hobbes rejects the notion that sovereignty could ever be divided among three estates. In *Behemoth* he argues that the theory of "mixed" monarchy was, in fact, one of the causes of the civil war in England. He castigates Charles's advisors for advocating such a position which only resulted, he states, in a halfhearted effort to win the war because of royalist fears that a complete victory for Charles would have destroyed the mixed monarchy.[20]

Hobbes's *Leviathan*

Hobbes's *Leviathan* (1651) is as radical a departure from the assumptions of previous political theories as is Machiavelli's *The Prince*. Hobbes constructs a political system based not upon historical precedent or theology, but upon psychological and sociological assumptions, upon an examination of human nature. Government is something which is made by men and caused by the nature of man. Man is thus the subject of the first book of *Leviathan*. Hobbes argues that since all men share the passions—but not necessarily the objects to which they are attached—to examine one man is to examine all. He divides the passions, the origins of all voluntary motion, into appetites and aversions. Whatever is an object of man's appetite is good; whatever is an object of man's aversion is evil. Good and evil are not then moral absolutes; they are defined, at this stage in Hobbes's argument, with reference to the desires and fears of the individual. The appetites of men continually change, and they differ from one man to another. Furthermore, appetites are incessant and felicity for man consists in achieving one's desires. Finally, appetites are of different strengths in different men.

The problem comes when man must exist in relation to other men, for if all men seek to attain their desires, there will be inevitable conflict between the desires of one man and the desires of all other men. Since men are basically equal in nature, all men have an equal hope of attaining the objects of their appetites. As a result, men who do not live within a commonwealth live in a natural condition of war, a perpetual struggle of competing appetites. Behavior is entirely motivated by self-interest. The consequence is that "every man is Enemy to every man" and all men live in "continuall feare" with the danger of "violent death." The life of man outside of a civil state is "solitary, poore, nasty, brutish, and short."[21]

From this, Hobbes advances two fundamental rules of reason: man ought to seek peace and ought to be willing "to lay down this right to all things; and be contented with so much liberty against other men, as he would allow other men against himselfe."[22] These laws, however, without something or someone to enforce them, are contrary to man's passions and hence do not and cannot guarantee peace. It is therefore essential that there be some form of common coercive power strong enough to enforce these covenants. This necessity leads to Hobbes's theories on the nature of civil government—the second part of *Leviathan*, "Of Commonwealth."

A commonwealth originates when a plurality of individuals agree that a single man or an assembly of men is given the right to represent them all. This representative power is called the sovereign; everyone else is a subject. Although the sovereign derives his power from this series of individual covenants between subjects, he himself does not enter into a covenant with his subjects. This one-sided relationship gives the sovereign absolute power over his subjects. Hobbes then details the rights which belong to the sovereign: he can do nothing which constitutes a reason which would free his subjects from their covenants; he cannot commit injustice or injury since by their covenants his actions are their actions; he is sole judge of what is necessary for the peace and defense of his subjects and is free to act accordingly; he is sole lawmaker and alone determines what is good and what is evil; and finally, he has the right of all judicature, the right to make war and peace, the right to maintain and command an army, and the right to choose all his counselors, ministers, magistrates, and officers. In short, the sovereign is supreme. There can be no such thing as a mixed or limited monarchy. Although men might object to the potential danger of such unlimited power, it is the only way that men can avoid living in an even worse condition—the state of nature.

In parts three and four of *Leviathan*, "Of a Christian Commonwealth" and "Of the Kingdom of Darkness," Hobbes deals with the relationship between religion and the state. Hobbes's sovereign is supreme not only in temporal matters but also in spiritual ones. He can be so for Hobbes because there are no moral absolutes: "These words of Good, Evill, and Contemptible, are ever used with relation to the person that useth them: There being nothing simply or absolutely so; nor any common Rule of Good and Evill, to be taken from the nature of the objects themselves."[23] Good and evil are determined and defined by the civil law and civil law is made by the sovereign. Even scriptual law derives its authority only through the sanction of the sovereign: "Those books [of the Bible] only are Canonicall, that is, Law, in every nation, which are established for such by the Soveraign Authority."[24] In Hobbes's commonwealth, the sovereign is supreme in all matters related to religion; he, like Moses, is "the sole Messenger of God, and Interpreter of His Commandements."[25] Since matters of religion are determined by the sovereign, it follows that there is no "universall Church as all Christians are bound to obey," for this would cut across the authority of individual sovereigns. Moreover, there is no split between spiritual and temporal government for there is "no other Government in this life, neither of State, nor Religion, but Temporall."[26]

Clarendon's Reply

Clarendon began writing *A Brief View and Survey of the Dangerous and pernicious Errors to Church and State, in Mr. Hobbes's Book, Entitled LEVIATHAN* during his final exile. Contact between Clarendon and Hobbes had extended over a number of years. While still in Jersey in 1646–48, Clarendon had read and disapproved of Hobbes's *De Cive*. He notes in *A Brief View* (7-8) that he had had a chance to read a small portion of *Leviathan* as it was being printed and that he had received a copy very soon after it was published in 1651. Clarendon's hostility toward *Leviathan* continued over the years. He wrote to Dr. John Barwick from Brussels on 25 July 1659, trying to persuade him to get Matthew Wren to write a reply to it: "Mr. *Hobbs* is my old Friend; yet I cannot absolve him from the Mischief he hath done to the King, the Church, the Laws, and the Nation."[27] What bothered Clarendon was that those published replies which he had seen had concentrated on the theoretical, or the philosophical, or the religious, or the scientific aspects of Hobbes's arguments.[28] What was really needed was to expose the fundamental political errors which *Leviathan* contained.

The scope of Clarendon's book is clearly indicated in its title, "the Dangerous and pernicious Errors to Church and State." This reply seeks to explore and expose the pragmatic implications to civil government of Hobbes's ideas. Although Clarendon touches from time to time upon what might be called philosophical errors in Hobbes's views, his approach is more practical than theoretical. This is, of course, exactly what one would expect, for Clarendon was not a philosopher but a shrewd and experienced statesman. He concentrates on those things "hurtful to the Peace and Policy of the Kingdom, or prejudicial to the sincerity of Religion" (16).

The book was finished at Montpellier in April 1670; the Dedication to Charles II is signed from Moulins, 10 May 1673. The exigencies of government had, no doubt, prevented Clarendon from undertaking a reply at an earlier date. More than this, though, Clarendon's reasons are quite clear from the "Epistle Dedicatory" where he writes that he could not "think of any thing in my power to perform of more importance to your Majesties service, then to answer Mr. *Hobbes's Leviathan*, and confute the doctrine therein contain'd, so pernicious to the Soveraign Power of Kings, and destructive to the affection and allegiance of Subjects" (ii–iii). Whether or not Charles ever read *A Brief View* is uncertain. It is likely, however, that Charles would have been more sympathetic to Hobbes's theory of sovereignty than Clarendon's. The manuscript was apparently carried back to England by Clarendon's son Laurence. There is a letter in the Clarendon correspondence from Clarendon to his eldest son Henry, Lord Cornbury, dated 17 March 1673, in which he asks for criticism of the manuscript (*Clarendon State Papers*, 3:supplement xlii–xliv). It was published at Oxford in 1676.

Reduced to their simplest terms, Clarendon's objections to Hobbes's theories are two-fold: first, government did not, at any time, or in any place, evolve in the manner in which Hobbes outlines; secondly, even if one granted Hobbes his covenant theory (which Clarendon does not), a government constructed upon such absolutist principles could not possibly work. Both are simple but significant criticisms. *Leviathan* is an important philosophical document but judged by realistic or workable political standards, Clarendon argues, it amounts to the product of a misguided theorist who knows nothing about the operations of government. As an experienced statesman, Clarendon is not interested in a philosophical construct, but in a workable reality.

In answer to Hobbes's theoretical generation of a commonwealth, Clarendon offers his version of how government was originally instituted. "Originally," for Clarendon, means beginning with Adam. His historical perspective is medieval and theological. He begins by rejecting Hobbes's view that outside of civil states man exists in a natural condition of war. Nothing is more contrary to the "honor and dignity" of God than to imagine such a thing. God gave man reason and other "noble Faculties" (27) so that he had the "natural strength and power to govern the World with peace and order" (67). Man began, then, not in a state of war, but a state of peace, and Adam was the "sole monarch" of the world. This absolute monarchy experienced neither "sedition" nor "civil war" until after the Flood. Then, when the generations of Noah had spread over the Earth, the nature of monarchy changed. Sovereigns started to act less paternally and to look on those they governed as "their mere subjects, not as their Allies" (69). This exercise of absolute power grew until the rulers realized that such an abuse must inevitably end in "absolute weakness" for if the people are treated as slaves rather than as subjects, they will not long support such a government: "Subjects should find profit and comfort in obeying, as well as Kings pleasure in commanding" (71). Rulers consequently found it necessary to restrict their powers, to grant "condescentions, concessions, and contracts" (71) to their subjects. Thus sovereignty, for Clarendon, is not derived from any type of contract, but rather from that original power invested in Adam by God. The obvious deduction from such a theory, but one which

Clarendon does not draw, is, as John Bowle has observed, that
Clarendon "seriously believed...that Charles I...possessed
authority from Adam."[29]

Clarendon's theory of government is a very conservative, Tudor
paternalism. Although there is no explicit mention of the divine
right of kings theory, Clarendon clearly does believe in several of its
tenets. By tracing monarchy back to Adam, Clarendon points to the
"divine" origins of such a form of government. In answer to
Hobbes's argument that a monarch, even one who had the "sovereignty from a descent of six hundred years," was a representative of
the people, Clarendon counters that a king is a king by reason of the
descent of sovereignty and that a king knows "too well the original
of his own power, to be contented to be thought the Representative
of the People" (57). To be a representative is to base sovereignty
upon an arbitrary foundation—the consent of the governed.
Rather, a king's majesty is "inherent in his office, and neither one
or the other is conferred upon him by the people" (59).

Even though Hobbes had based sovereignty upon covenant, he
accords the sovereign complete power; he alone makes and repeals
laws. A law does not remain a law because of custom or length of
time, but because of the will of the sovereign. In this way Hobbes
had, for example, eliminated the concept of common law. Clarendon agrees that the sovereign is sole legislator. It is his "stamp, and
Royal consent" that makes advice and counsel into law, but once
made, a law cannot be repealed or declared void at the whim of the
sovereign. A sovereign is obliged to observe it: "He cannot break it,
or absolve himself from the observation of it, without violation of
justice" (122). The role of Parliament is to offer advice "humbly"
(58); the concept of a divided authority is nonsense: "*That the
power was divided between the King, and the Lords, and the House
of Commons*...was an opinion never heard of in *England* till the
Rebellion was begun" (54). The rebellion, in fact, resulted not from
any "defect" in the laws, nor any "defect of the just and ample
power of the King," but rather from the power-hungry men who
"suppressed the strength of the Laws, and wrested the power out of
the hands of the King" (54).

The point to which Clarendon keeps returning, however, is that by granting the sovereign such unlimited powers, Hobbes has, paradoxically, weakened rather than strengthened the sovereign's authority over his subjects. The idea that a sovereign does not enter into a convenant with his subjects is ridiculous. What would prevent the people from using force against a ruler who declares himself exempt from all "Oaths, Covenants, and Promises" (48)? Anyway, a sovereign who has no covenant with his people has no security for their obedience.

So absolute is the power of the sovereign in *Leviathan* that the liberty of his subjects consists only in those things which he permits. But Clarendon asks how such an absolute power could exist. Subjects could not and would not support a sovereign when he is capable of taking everything from them; such an idea would result in civil war rather than prevent it. Nothing is more absurd than to imagine that such a system would be realistic. Furthermore, at the same time that he gives the sovereign this power, Hobbes totally undermines it by allowing certain circumstances under which a subject may refuse to obey. These instances arise, Hobbes noted, from those "rights" which cannot be transferred by the social covenant which established government. Specifically, a man does not transfer his natural rights to defend himself against death, wounds, or imprisonment, and, most importantly, the obligation of a subject to his sovereign lasts only as long as the sovereign has the power to protect him, for the "end of Obedience is Protection." As Clarendon points out, such a principle allows subjects the right to withdraw their obedience at the very times (e.g., invasion) that their ruler has most need of their assistance.

Another of the results of granting the sovereign such unlimited power was to eliminate essentially the concept of private property. The sovereign has a right to everything. Government, even civilization itself, Clarendon replies, cannot function or exist where there is no guarantee of private property:

> Whatsoever is of Civility and good Manners, all that is of Art and Beauty, or of real and solid Wealth in the World, is...the child of

beloved Propriety; and they who would strangle this Issue, desire to demolish all Buildings, eradicate all Plantations, to make the Earth barren, and man-kind to live again in Tents, and nurish his Cattle by successive marches into those Fields where the grass grows. Nothing but the joy in Propriety reduc'd us from this barbarity; and nothing but security in the same, can preserve us from returning into it again. (111)

Clarendon even goes further. A wise sovereign will not arbitrarily tax his subjects. The consideration for Clarendon is again a practical one: Won't a sovereign be stronger by accepting what his subjects are willing to give instead of "letting them know that they have nothing to give, because all they have is his" (177)? Even supposing that subjects might refuse to contribute to their own preservation (and such a case has never happened), most rulers would rather hazard such a possibility than allow the sovereign the legal right to everything his subjects possess. Such a condition would lead only to "perpetual inquietude and vexation," and, Clarendon concludes, we know the effects of fear too well to think that anyone who is "in a continual fright can be fix'd in a firm obedience" (180).

When Clarendon turns to exposing the "dangerous and pernicious" errors in parts three and four of *Leviathan*, he changes his method of approach. Although he is appalled by Hobbes's treatment of scripture, by his embarking on a "Sea of new and extravagant interpretations... without any other autority then of his own ungovern'd fancy" (202), Clarendon does not attempt to refute Hobbes's glosses and interpretations. A writer such as Hobbes, Clarendon concludes, exposes religion to the "irreverent examination of dissolute persons" and prostitutes the "sacred mysteries of our Faith... to a Philosophical and Mathematical inquistion" (200). Given such an attitude, it is not surprising that Clarendon carefully avoids any direct confrontation with Hobbes over theological issues. He does not, for example, comment on Hobbes's nominalism or materialism. His objections are those of a conservative, and uncritical, Christian. Good and evil are moral absolutes; the authority of the scriptures is unquestioned. The idea of making either controlled by the sovereign is an impious fancy concocted by Hobbes.

Essentially, Clarendon confines his reply to an examination of the relationship which should exist between Church and State. On this matter, Clarendon and Hobbes are not so opposed. Clarendon agrees, for example, that there is no one church which has authority to control all Christians. Such an idea, for Clarendon, who like Hobbes associates it with the papacy, is an "extravagant and sense-less" notion that is unsupported by either scripture or historical precedent. Clarendon also agrees that any distinction or separation between temporal and spiritual power only serves to undermine the sovereign's authority by allowing subjects to profess subjection or obedience to a "Foreign Power and Jurisdiction" (233). The extent and nature of the ecclesiastical power left by Christ to his Apostles was only a power to "proclaim," "perswade," and "teach": they were given no "external, ordinary, coercive power." Such a function, however, can only be fulfilled by "publishing and explain-ing the Scriptures." In this way the clergy are "obliged to declare and teach the Doctrine of Christ before the Doctrine of the King" (247). Clarendon does not see this necessity as in any way impairing the sovereignty of a ruler, for he [the ruler] is "obliged to take care that the Laws and Precepts of God his Soveraign be punctually submitted to" (248). Moreover, there is no real power conflict here, for in England at least, Clarendon continues: "There is neither Bishop nor Priest who pretends to any Power or Jurisdiction, inconsistent with the Kings Supremacy, in Ecclesiastical as well as Temporal matters" (249).

Clarendon is clearly aware of one final implication of Hobbes's argument on secular power over religious matters. In his earlier *De Cive*, Hobbes allowed his sovereign power the right to determine what the nature of the commonwealth's religion would be, but had also indicated that it would be Christian. In *Leviathan*, though, Hobbes offers no similar caution. There is no guarantee that the uniform religion imposed by the sovereign will be Christian and the subject is obliged to obey his sovereign regardless of his own private beliefs. Hobbes had posed two questions: "What... if a

King, or a Senate, or other Soveraign Person forbids us to beleeve in Christ?" and "What if wee bee commanded by our lawfull Prince, to say with our tongue, wee beleeve not?" "Profession with the tongue," replies Hobbes, "is but an externall thing."[30] To license such hypocrisy, writes Clarendon, is a "monstrous Impiety." Furthermore, Hobbes's assertion carries a very great moral danger in that "he who is a Christian in his heart, & upon any Kings commands shall profess with his Tongue that he doth not believe in Christ, will not be admitted by our Saviour to be of his Church" (251). Concluding his defense of Christianity, Clarendon asserts: "He cannot confess him with his mouth, that doth not believe him in his heart; and he doth not believe him in his heart to no purpose, that will not confess him with his mouth. A man cannot be a true Christian without both" (252).

Clarendon's reply to *Leviathan* really addresses only the pragmatic implications of Hobbes's theories as they relate to government and to the church. The theoretical aspects of *Leviathan* did not directly concern Clarendon. There is, in fact, an extent to which a man such as Clarendon—a man literally, historically, and pragmatically minded—could not understand Hobbes at all. As we saw in chapter 4, Clarendon was interested in history and political maxims only to the extent to which they illuminated the events and behavior of the present. On religious matters his thought was extremely conventional and conservative. At a number of places in his reply Clarendon pauses to speculate on Hobbes's motives in writing such a book. He concedes, at least, no other one than a desire to undermine the traditional basis of government in England (and hence to ingratiate himself with Cromwell) and a genuine ignorance on Hobbes's part of the operations of government. *Leviathan*, he concludes, is a real threat to civil peace: "I never read any Book that contains in it so much Sedition, Treason, and Impiety as this *Leviathan*; and therefore ... it is very unfit to be read, taught, or sold, as dissolving all the ligaments of Government, and undermining all principles of Religion" (319). As for the correction of Hobbes and his "theorem of politics," nothing would be as effective as to give Hobbes a little practical experience:

I should be very glad that Mr. *Hobbes* might have a place in Parliament, and sit in Counsel, and be present in Courts of Justice, and other Tribunals; whereby it is probable he would find, that his solitary cogitation, how deep soever, and his too peremptory adhering to some Philosophical Notions, and even Rules of Geometry, had misled him in the investigation of Policy... And possibly this might, and I doubt only could, prevail upon him, to make such recollection and acknowledgment of all the falshood, profaneness, impiety, and blasphemy in his Book. (322)

Chapter Seven

Clarendon's Religion of State

In addition to his *History of the Rebellion* and *A Brief Survey*, Clarendon wrote two other books in his final exile, both of which deal with the relationship between church and state. The first, composed at some point during 1672 to 1673, was *Animadversions Upon a Book, Intituled; Fanaticism Fanatically Imputed to the Catholick Church*, a book related to a series of exchanges between Edward Stillingfleet, a minor but prolific Anglican divine, and Serenus Cressy, a convert to Catholicism. The second, the product of a number of years of reading, but apparently finished between 1673 and early 1674, was *Religion and Policy and the Countenance and Assistance each should give to the other*, essentially, despite its title, a history of the papacy.

Clarendon was not a theologian, any more than he was a political philosopher. Rather, his interest in religion was always related to politics, to the interaction between religion and civil government. In his *History* he had remarked: "The ecclesiastical and civil state was so wrought and interwoven together, and, in truth, so incorporated in each other, that, like Hippocrates' twins, they cannot but laugh and cry together" (4:40). What Clarendon opposed was any claim to an ecclesiastical authority independent of civil control. To this extent, he, like all Church of England men, was an Erastian.[1] It was this attitude that accounted in large part for his hostility toward Presbyterianism, which upheld the autonomy of the Kirk, and toward Roman Catholicism, which placed obedience to the Pope above obedience to the civil sovereign. The Presbyterian threat had passed with the restoration of Charles II, but the Catholic had not. Both of these two works center around the claims of papal supremacy and their implications for the civil sovereign.

Either book could probably have been written at almost any point in Clarendon's life. The views that they espouse are Clarendonian commonplaces that recur at a number of points in many of his previous books and pamphlets. The fact that they are written during the final exile appears to be related to a personal event. Clarendon's daughter Anne had married James, the Duke of York, in September 1660. While still in exile both James and Anne were attracted to the Roman church. At some undated point between 1660 and 1671, James converted, although it was not publically acknowledged until 1673. Clarendon had long been aware of the Roman sympathies of both Charles II and James. Charles was, of course, without legitimate heir; he would be succeeded by his brother; and if James converted, England would have a Catholic king. The possibility frightened Clarendon but the threat must have seemed even more real when in 1670 Clarendon received the news that his daughter was rumored to have converted. He wrote private letters immediately, to both the duke and duchess. Apparently he assumed that the duke was not a convert (or at least he took that particular rhetorical tact). He urged James to use his "authority" to keep his wife firm to her faith in the Church of England, pointing out the dangerous political implications that such a conversion would occasion:

It is not possible your Royal Highness can be without Zeal, and entire devotion for that Church, for the purity and preservation whereof your blessed father made himself a sacrifice; and to the restoration whereof you have contributed so much yourself, and which highly deserves the King's protection and yours, since there can be no possible defection in the hearts of the people, whilst due reverence is made to the Church (*Clarendon State Papers*, 3:supplement xxxvii)

Similarly, he upbraided Anne: "You bring irreparable dishonour, scandal and prejudice to the Duke your husband, to whom you ought to pay all imaginable duty, and who, I presume, is much more precious to you than your own life; and all possible ruin to your children" (*Clarendon State Papers*, 3:supplement xl). The threat which Clarendon saw was not theological or theoretical, but political and practical. The specter of a Catholic king for England loomed in Clarendon's mind. Clarendon's reaction was heightened by his position—former advisor to two kings, restorer of the English church, father to the duchess—but it was not in any way untypical. In order to understand the nature and depth of Clarendon's reaction to this threat, it is necessary to trace briefly the English Protestant view of Catholicism.

English Protestants and Anti-Catholicism

The threat which Clarendon, like other English Protestants, saw in Catholicism was more political than it was doctrinal. It aroused fears of persecution, of rebellion against the sovereign, of absolutism. Such fears were unjustifiable, indeed, even irrational. But they gripped the English Protestant imagination because of a number of factors.

One particularly formative influence was the memory of the persecution of Protestants under the reign of Queen Mary. When Mary ascended the throne in 1553 she believed that God wanted her to restore the true Church and, most importantly, that heretics were agents of the devil. Hundreds of suspected heretics were examined and imprisoned. Many Protestants fled England; others were burned at the stake. The burnings started in February 1555 and by the time it was over some three years later, an estimated 300 heretics had died. They included 5 bishops, about 100 priests, and some 60 women. Some recanted, but others died singing hymns. Instead of reestablishing Catholicism in England, Mary provided the link between popery and persecution. Should a Catholic ever again assume the throne, Protestant England would undergo a similar trial. The Marian persecutions lived on in English memory in part because of John Foxe's *Acts and Monuments*, more commonly known as the "Book of Martyrs," the first English edition appearing in 1563 during the reign of Elizabeth. Foxe placed the Marian martyrs in the tradition of the persecution of "true" Christians which stretched from the earliest martyrs to the time of his book.

The reign of Elizabeth brought a Protestant restoration. With the Act of Supremacy, Elizabeth was declared "the only supreme governor of this realm, as well as in all spiritual and ecclesiastical things or causes as temporal." The Act of Uniformity restored the Prayer Book of 1552 with some changes; the vacant bishropics were filled; the Protestant exiles flocked back to England. But the fears of Protestants were rekindled on 25 February 1570, when Pope Pius V issued his bull *Regnans in Excelsis* which declared Elizabeth a bastard who forfeited her right to the throne. Her subjects, on pain of excommunication, were no longer to obey her. Pius's intention, writes Stephen Neill, was "to encourage the English Roman Catholics to rise in rebellion against their lawful sovereign.... By a stroke of the pen the Pope of Rome had made every English Roman Catholic ... a potential traitor to his country and his Queen."[2] A. O. Meyer summarizes the significance of Pius's action for English Protestants: "No event in English history, not even the Gunpowder Plot, produced so deep and enduring an effect on England's attitude to the catholic church as the bull of Pius V. Englishmen never forgot their queen's excommunication.... The story of the excommunication, and of the pope who freed men from their oaths, and subjects from their allegiance, was a weapon that kept its edge for centuries and effectively put a stop to every thought of toleration for the Papists."[3] The threat was political and Elizabeth and her government responded in political terms. Catholics were potential traitors who sought to overthrow the English government; they, in turn, were persecuted on political rather than theological grounds. Lord Burghley, Elizabeth's chief minister, defended the execution of Roman Catholic priests: they were "traitors against their sovereign and queen in adhering to him [the Pope], being the notable and only open hostile enemy in all actions of war against Her Majesty, her kingdoms, and people."[4]

Plots against the established government, both real and imagined, were continually discovered which revealed the machinations of the Papists. The most famous came in 1605 in the reign of James I when a small group of English Roman Catholics plotted to blow up king, Lords, and Commons by exploding gunpowder stored in a basement under the houses of Parliament. Their hope was that in the inevitable confusion which followed they might be able to seize power. The powder was to have been fired by Guy Fawkes, a name which all Englishmen remember to this day.

By the reign of Charles I, things had become somewhat more complicated for the menace of Roman Catholicism now was seen as allied with the English monarchy. For one thing, Charles's queen, Henrietta Maria, was Catholic and she was free to practice her religion at court. Penal laws against Catholics were relaxed; a number of important government positions were held by Catholics. And to many an Englishman, the ritualism reintroduced into the Church of England by Archbishop Laud smacked of popery, as did his emphasis upon episcopal authority. For a period in the Long Parliament, the royal cause and Charles's absolutist actions seemed to many to be popish manifestations. The Grand Remonstrance from Commons in 1641 explicitly located the problem:

> The root of all this mischief we find to be a malignant and pernicious design of subverting the fundamental laws and principles of government, upon which the religion and justice of this kingdom are firmly established. The actors and promoters thereof have been:
> 1. The Jesuited Papists, who hate the laws, as the obstacles of that change and subversion of religion which they so much long for.
> 2. The bishops, and the corrupt part of the clergy, who cherish formality and superstition as the natural effects and more probable supports of their own ecclesiastical tyranny and usurpation.
> 3. Such councillors and courtiers as for private ends have engaged themselves to further the interests of some foreign princes or states to the prejudice of his Majesty and the State at home.[5]

The Roman Catholic enemy seemed on the verge of gaining control of the monarchy.

Charles moved, of course, to discredit any such ideas. On 10 August 1642 he issued a proclamation "inhibiting all Popish recusants, or any other who refused to take the oaths of allegiance and supremacy, to resort to his army, disclaiming the service of all such." Clarendon in his *History* goes on to explain the reason for the king's action: "It was very plain that the imputation raised by the Parliament upon the King, of an intention to bring in, or, which they thought all one, of conniving at and tolerating, Popery, did make a deep impression upon the people generally" (5:note to 441). As the war continued, the charges that Charles supported Popery lost their force. Any final doubts, writes John Miller, that "Charles I was a Papist in disguise were dispelled by his impeccably Anglican martyrdom."[6]

Throughout the interregnum Clarendon worked to keep Charles II true to his father's faith and free from any religious commitments, either Presbyterian or Roman Catholic, made in exchange for assistance toward his restoration. Restored to his throne, Charles II moved to secure for Catholics a degree of toleration and to suppress or remove some of the penal laws against them. Charles's sympathies with Roman Catholicism were widely known. His brother, James, heir-apparent to the throne, was a convert. These two factors, combined with the emergence of Louis XIV, regarded as "the epitome of absolutism and the greatest enemy of European Protestantism,"[7] charged the English air in the 1670s with fear. A Catholic king for England might well herald a return to the persecution of Mary's reign and a new era of absolutist rule. Clarendon's *Animadversions* and *Religion and Policy* are both products of this political climate rather than part of a continuing tradition of theological dispute between Protestant and Catholic theologians. Indeed, neither work is theoretical or even significant outside of the context of Clarendon's own thought on the interrelationships between Church and State.

Animadversions

At some point during 1672 to 1673, Clarendon wrote *Animadversions Upon a Book, Intituled; Fanaticism Fanatically Imputed to the Catholick Church*. The book is the fourth in a series of six exchanges between Edward Stillingfleet and Hugh Paulinus Cressy, although it is only tangentially related to their paper dispute. Part of the connection for Clarendon was personal. Cressy had been part of a small circle of friends who assembled at Great Tew, the country house of Lucius Cary, later Lord Falkland. That group, which Clarendon sketched at great length in his autobiography, had a distinctive theological bias perhaps best embodied in William Chillingworth's *The Religion of Protestants*.[8] That is, the Tew circle emphasized the essential simplicity of religious faith. What was necessary to be believed was obvious to all. Disputes and controversies centered around inessentials and were ultimately unresolvable by appeals to scripture, tradition, the authority of the Fathers, or that of Councils. The theology of the circle was both rationalistic and humanistic.[9]

Through Falkland, Cressy had obtained a canonry of Windsor in 1642, but with the outbreak of the Civil War, the seeming dissolution of the Church of England, and Falkland's death, Cressy moved to Paris, where he converted to Catholicism. Clarendon had been concerned over Cressy's conversion. In January 1647 he had written to Dr. John Earle: "It is a great loss to the Church, but a greater to his friends.... If we cannot keep him a Minister of our Church, I wish he would continue a lay-man in their's, which would somewhat lessen the defection, and it may be preserve a greater proportion of his innocence" (*Clarendon State Papers*, 2:322). Cressy, however, quickly lost his "innocence," publishing in 1647 his *Exomologesis*, which explained the "occasion and motives" of his conversion. Anthony à Wood notes: "This *Exomologesis* was the golden calf which the English papists fell down and worshipped. They brag'd that book to be unanswerable and to have given total overthrow to the Chillingworthians and book and tenets of Lucius Lord Falkland."[10] In 1649, Cressy became a Benedictine monk and assumed the name Serenus. Much later, in 1672, the tenets of Chillingworth and the Tew circle found expression in Edward Stillingfleet's *A Discourse Concerning the Idolatry Practised in the Church of Rome ... in answer to some Papers of a Revolted Protestant* [Cressy]."[11] Cressy's reply was *Fanaticism Fanatically Imputed to the Catholick Church by Doctour Stillingfleet*.[12] This in turn elicited both a reply from Stillingfleet and Clarendon's *Animadversions*[13]

The fourth part of Stillingfleet's *A Discourse* is entitled "Of the Fanaticism of the Roman Church." He begins with a definition of fanaticism: "Either an Enthusiastick way of Religion; or resisting authority, under a pretense of Religion."[14] To illustrate the first part of the definition, Stillingfleet cites such things as the "private revelations" of saints, the origins and nature of many of the religious orders, and particular devotional practices of the Church of Rome. The second part—"resisting authority"—is an attack on the Jesuits whose "principles and practices" are "as destructive to Government, as of the most Fanatick Sectaries, which ever have been among us."[15]

It is this fourth section that Cressy concentrates on in his *Fanaticism Fanatically Imputed*. Much of Cressy's reply is a defense of the saints, the orders, and such things as the contemplative life and the mystical experience. When he comes, however, to the second part of Stillingfleet's argument, Cressy returns the criticism, asserting that "all of Churches of Protestants, as they are Principled by him in his Book" practice "pure putrid Fanaticism."[16] The crux of Cressy's argument is one of Stillingfleet's "principles" of Protestantism: "No sober enquirer can miss of what is necessary for salvation; there can be no necessity supposed of any infallible society of men, either to attest, or explain these Writings among Christians."[17] Such a principle, Cressy retorts, makes every man his own teacher and judge of scripture. This is the real fanaticism for it invites every man to frame his own religion. Cressy criticizes Stillingfleet at some length for encouraging such a splintering of religious belief and practice, concluding his book with an analysis of the devices for unity which can be found in the Church of Rome.

Although there is much passing comment in *Animadversions* which relates to specific Catholic doctrines, practices, and history, Clarendon's principal concern is to "draw the dispute that is between the *Church* and the *Laws of England*, and his Majesties Subjects of his own Dominions who profess to be of the *Roman Faith*, into a narrower room, and within that compass that properly contains it"(9). That dispute, for Clarendon, centers on a single factor: English Catholics acknowledge the authority of the pope over that of the king. All of the other differences such as those on points of doctrine or practice are not crucial because only the essentials of Christianity are necessary for salvation and about these there are no disputes. Clarendon makes a distinction between "faith" and "religion." There is only one faith and that consists simply in the belief in Christ and his resurrection. Religion, on the other hand, is the "uniting, or the being united of pious men in the profession of that Faith, [and] may be exercised in *several* and *different forms*, and *ways*, and with *several ceremonies* according to the constitutions and rules of the *several Countries* and *Kingdoms* where it is practised" (128). Christ prescribed only the "essential principles": "Christ and his Apostles left their Declarations of what we are to believe, and what we are to do, so clearly stated, that we cannot *dangerously mistake*" (125). "There are no doubt many things fit to be known, and which we should be the better for knowing, which are not so manifest, but it is not so necessary if it be not manifest" (117). The idea that there is but *"one Church*, and *one Religion*, in which men may be saved" is an "artifice introduced to perplex mankind" for there is "room enough in Heaven for them all" (127-128).

This does not mean, though, that every man is free to frame his own religion, as Cressy charges. Rather, whatever unity there is within a religion is determined by the sovereign. The lines of Clarendon's argument here are more clearly and fully stated in *Religion and Policy* (see below). Religion thus becomes "religion of state," for it is the sovereign who best knows how to establish "such *forms*, and *ceremonies* and *circumstances* in what pertains to Religion, as are most agreeable to the nature, and inclination, and disposition of a people" (136). The essential difference between the Church of England and the Church of Rome is reduced to a question of where authority is placed to which obedience is owed: "We of the *Church of England* hold ours to be due to the *King*, the *Church*, and the *Law*: Mr. Cressy would have us pay it to the *Pope*, which we cannot submit to, not because he is *fallible*, but because he is not a *Magistrate* who hath any jurisdiction over us" (110).

As far as a universal unity of doctrine and practice such as is envisioned by the Church of Rome, it is impossible. Controversies over inessential matters are a waste of time for there is no authority, other than that of the sovereign, by which to settle such debates. The Church of England, like that of Rome, believes in the authority of tradition, but only where tradition is "universal and uncontradicted." Tradition, though, is too often uncertain for a Church always to be guided and governed by it. Similarly, the Church of England has a great respect for the writings of the Fathers but, "neither they [Catholics] nor we, nor any other Christian Church in the World, do submit or concur in all that the *Fathers* have taught, who were never all of *one mind*, and therefore may very lawfully have *their reasons* examined by the *reasons of other men*" (189). The only practical type of religious unity is national and even that should be determined only by what is most conducive to preserving the peace. "No *Reformation*," Clarendon cautions, "is worth the charge of a *Civil War*" (136).

Clarendon concludes *Animadversions* with a series of nine significant questions which would form the basis of a real exchange between the two churches. As might be expected, each centers around Clarendon's idea of "religion of state." If only these "particulars" which are "warily declined" or "very perfunctorily handled" by the defenders of the Church of Rome were fully discussed, then "the *foundation, doctrine* and *discipline* of that Church, would be in a short time utterly overthrown and demolished, or worthily vindicated and supported" (255).

Religion and Policy

The full title of this work—*Religion and Policy and the Countenance and Assistance each should give to the other. With a Survey of the power and jurisdiction of the Pope in the dominions of other princes*—implies that it is basically theoretical, that it is a full examination of the nature and extent of the interaction of religion and government. Such, however, is not the case, for the work is principally devoted to what, to judge at least from its title, seems a secondary concern—that is, a survey of the power and jurisdiction of the papacy. Clarendon traces in great detail the papal succession from St. Peter through Clement X (elected 1670), concentrating on the origins and development of the papal claim to "supreme jurisdiction" in both spiritual and temporal matters.

Clarendon's work on *Religion and Policy* extended over a considerable period of time. In the "Continuation" of his autobiography, he records that he began a work on the "Superiority and Supremacy of the Pope" while in Spain in 1650-51 after reading Gonzalo de Illescas's *Historia Pontifical y Catholica* and several other volumes on "pontifical history." He returned to the work soon after he left England for his final exile. Among other manuscripts which have survived is a list of popes with some factual notations which Clarendon apparently compiled in 1667 with a later addition for Clement X in 1670 and extensive notes from an edition of the *Bullarium Romanum* which are dated 1672-73.[18] The manuscript of *Religion and Policy* itself is in the handwriting of William Shaw, Clarendon's secretary, and is dated at the end from Moulins, 12 February 1674.[19]

In the Introduction Clarendon asserts: "The sovereign care protection and propagation of Christian religion are committed by God to the Christian kings and princes" (1). This is proved in two ways. First, there is God's own declaration concerning the Church recorded in Isaiah: "Kings shall be thy nursing fathers, and queens thy nursing mothers." Secondly, reason itself dictates that religion can only be protected and fostered by those "who have authority to give laws to their subjects, to which they are bound to submit, and power to cause those laws to be executed, if they refuse to submit to them" (1). This does not mean that the sovereign can impose whatever religion he wishes, for that has been established by God, but it does mean that the sovereign is free to alter the "forms" and "circumstances" for the improvement and propagation of religion.

Such externals are not "prescribed" or "directed" by scripture, and the sovereign, acting with the assistance of "learned and pious persons," is free to make changes, assuming that such changes are made with consideration for the "peace and prosperity" of government and for the "nature and humour of the people, [and] the custom and disposition of the time" (3). Thus the externals of religion vary from nation to nation and from one historical period to another. Hence it follows that it is a practical impossibility to impose a uniform system of externals on all of Christianity. This freedom of form does not mean that "private and particular" men are free to choose for themselves the most appealing practice. This decision is left only to the sovereign and once he decides, it is legally necessary to conform to the prescribed pattern. It is only by such authority, Clarendon concludes, that "unity and uniformity (which are very wholesome if not necessary ingredients unto peace) may be established by every prince in his particular dominions" (5).

It would be impossible to summarize the vast scope of Clarendon's history of the papacy. He treats the popes in chronological order, concentrating almost exclusively on the political aspects of each reign and its interactions with the civil powers of England and Europe. Rarely does Clarendon touch upon doctrinal matters and even then only if the example is sufficiently ludicrous or pernicious to rhetorically undercut papal power and jurisdiction. What is interesting, though, about *Religion and Policy* is not its accuracy but rather its technique. The basis of Clarendon's arguments are never theoretical; they are historical. He refutes papal claims to a jurisdiction by examining what in fact has happened in the past.

The first section of *Religion and Policy* surveys the succession, election, and jurisdiction of the popes from St. Peter to Paul V (elected 1605). Catholic controversalists had sought to establish the Church's claims to supremacy in part by the assertion and demonstration of continuity—an unbroken succession of authority transmitted from St. Peter. Clarendon turns first to the historical evidence which supports such a claim. Almost all of what we know about the early popes and even their order of succession is derived not from original documents, but from later histories. Hence, Clarendon observes, "There is not only no authority that obliges, but no reason that persuades us, to believe any thing positively in the transactions of the church or of churchmen" (12). Further, considering the civil persecution under which these early popes lived, it is certain that the concept of jurisdiction meant little. And from what we know of the election and succession of the early popes, it is clear that during this period "there was no form prescribed for the election, nor any persons appointed or who pretended power to elect" (19). Moreover, we must "reasonably suppose" that a "constant rule" would have been dictated by God "if our Saviour had ever intended that the Bishop of Rome should be the sole monarch of the Church" (27). The history of papal succession has been so marked by political interference, intrigue, and even overt control that "no serious man can look upon the transactions as relating to religion" (36).

The second section of *Religion and Policy*, which comprises the overwhelming majority of the text, is a survey of "papal usurpations." Clarendon argues that the emergence of papal supremacy was closely tied to political expediency. Civil sovereigns appealed to the pope for political support against both their own people and their neighbors; the pope in turn extended his power and jurisdiction through such opportunities. The temporal nature of this support for the pope, as opposed to his inherent and derived spiritual authority, is evidenced as well in the often barbarous treatment which successive popes had at the hands of either the people or a particular sovereign. Here, Clarendon carefully catalogs examples of popes who were imprisoned, tortured, or executed by the temporal power and many instances in which sovereigns exercised complete control over papal policies, decisions, and elections.

Although Clarendon's treatment of the interaction between the major European powers and the papacy is quite detailed, his principal concern is with England. He is careful to discredit firmly any possible claims of papal jurisdiction within England which are based upon historical precedents. Contrary to the claims of papal historians, Christianity was brought to England by Joseph of Arimathea before St. Peter even came to Rome (18). Thus the pope has no claim to jurisdiction on historical grounds. It is true that Rome achieved a certain amount of authority in England during, for example, the reigns of Henry I and Henry II, but that was not because of the "constitution of the kingdom, or any preadmitted power of the pope formerly incorporated into the laws of the land" (123), but rather because both kings found this external assistance politically expedient internally. Pope Innocent III exercised "wanton" jurisdiction in England during the reign of King John but again "whatever the Pope got then in England is to be imputed to the guilt and weakness of the King, not to the consent of the time" (141). The price that John paid for the pope's protection involved essentially divesting himself of "all manner of sovereignty" in such a way that he "might be truly and literally called the Pope's

Beadsman" (146). Innocent, in turn, absolved John "from the observation of all oaths" made to his subjects and excommunicated anyone who should "presume to rebel against him" (147).

Such behavior is only an example of what, for Clarendon, is the most pernicious power claimed by the pope—the authority to interfere in what were essentially legal matters:

I am persuaded, if there were a short collection of the bulls and dispensations they have granted... for the dissolving and making of marriages, the breaking of oaths and lawful contracts, and for absolving of prejuries, and the like, they would be found to have introduced more mischief into the Christian world, and to have brought more scandal upon Christian religion, than all the heretics whom they have condemned from the time of the Apostles. (193)

Clarendon also cites significant acts of limitation of papal authority and jurisdiction during the reigns of Edward I, Edward III, Richard II, Henry IV, and Henry VI, none of which could have occurred if the "primacy of jurisdiction of the Pope had been acknowledged in England" (240).

One of the most important moments in the relationship between England and Rome came with Henry VIII's attempts to divorce Katherine of Aragon. On the morality of the issue, Clarendon is the loyal royal servant. Henry's faults can be traced to the "vice" of age. Many men merely "out of hope of issue" procured divorces and the Church did make "too much merchandise of it" (319). Largely because of the pressures exerted by Emperor Charles V, the nephew of Henry's wife, the pope was forced to excommunicate Henry in a "frantic" bull full of "imperious, insolent, profane, and tyrannical expressions" (322). The act, however, went ignored in the Catholic world, for there was not "one Catholic Prince in Europe who did not with the same warmth embrace and desire his friendship that they had done before" nor did "one of his Catholic subjects withdraw his allegiance from him, either clergy or laity, upon the stroke of that thunderbolt" (322).

The act which most clearly represented the threat that Catholicism poses to the civil authority was the excommunication of

Elizabeth by Pope Pius V. As noted earlier, on 25 February 1570 Pius issued his bull of excommunication, *Regnans in Excelsis*. In it he declared Elizabeth to be guilty of heresy and of encouraging heresy. Since she had therefore forfeited her "pretended right" to the English throne, it absolved all her subjects from "oaths of fidelity" to her. Faced with such overt aggression, it is no wonder, Clarendon observes, that Elizabeth provided "the strictest laws against the emissaries of such a tyrannical usurper, and against all those who, submitting to his authority, were like to conspire with them against her person" (424).

Pius's initial actions against Elizabeth were carried even further by his successor Gregory XIII. It was under Gregory that the Catholic Church encouraged the implementation of the logical consequence of Pius's excommunication of Elizabeth. Clarendon cites the example of Dr. William Parry, who during the winter of 1583-84 approached the Papal Nuncio in Madrid, proposing to kill Elizabeth. A plenary indulgence was obtained, satisfying Parry, in Clarendon's words, that "it was lawful to kill the Queen, provided that it was not out of malice, or for revenge, but only out of charity, and for the advancement of Catholic religion" (442) and granting absolution if he died while performing the assassination. Clarendon's statement here is somewhat misleading and, indeed, all the facts surrounding Parry remain uncertain today. It is not clear, for example, that Parry's plan involved assassination. The undertaking was, in A. O. Meyer's words, "to restore England to obedience to the Holy See." But Meyer continues, "according to the idea then prevalent in Rome, this 'restoration' could only be effected by putting Elizabeth out of the way." Despite the particular situation involving Parry, however, there is certain evidence that during this period the official papal attitude was as Clarendon represents it, that it would be "lawful" (not a sin) to kill Elizabeth providing it was done for "religious" reasons.[20]

As this example proves, Clarendon argues, the pope's claim to supreme spiritual authority represents a constant threat to civil order, for he asks Catholics to acknowledge only half (the temporal part) of the obedience which Protestant subjects pay to their king. The sovereign must, as a result of this divided loyalty, give Catholics only half of the normal protection and must also enact strict laws to prevent his Catholic subjects from being in a position in which they can do any "hurt" to either king or country. A sovereign who has no guarantee of the loyalty and obedience of every subject cannot govern securely and effectively.

Clarendon will not agree to any separation of jurisdiction—that is, that the pope can claim spiritual jurisdiction and the sovereign temporal. For Clarendon, the two are inextricably bound and both belong to the civil power. The phrase "spiritual authority" has never been defined and it has, in the past, inevitably led to intervention in and direction of temporal affairs. Surely, Clarendon concludes, there is no power more "odious and formidable" to sovereigns. Princes cannot allow their subjects to be "corrupted" by such a doctrine; they must identify and punish or restrict anyone who refuses to renounce the pope's claims.

If only the Roman Catholic laity and clergy will foreswear their independence upon Rome and agree to live under the laws of the kingdom, then the state can by degrees repeal those "severe and rigid" penalties under which they must now live. Clarendon has no desire to convert all Catholics to Protestantism or to prevent them from the exercise of their religion—such ideas would be neither "agreeable to policy nor to piety." But if only the Roman Catholics will agree to exclude the pope's claims of spiritual jurisdiction, then they can be granted the "common privileges" of subjects. The state, in turn, should then provide "ecclesiastical teachers, of the mildest and most peaceable dispositions" (709). Such a plan, he concludes, would remove the "uncharitableness" which inevitably accompanies religious faction: "When no mischievous action doth necessarily result from our opinions, how erroneous soever, we should be no more offended with each other for those differences, than for the distinct colour of our eyes, or hair" (711).

What emerges from these two books is a clear statement of Clarendon's view of religion. For Clarendon only the essentials of Christianity were necessary for salvation and about these there was no controversy. Unity of doctrine and practice was impossible; the best that could be hoped for was a national unity, "a religion of

state." Even on the national level, though, Clarendon felt that
specific determination of "inessential" matters must be made with
consideration to what was most conducive to civil peace. In *Animadversions* he had warned: "No *Reformation* is worth the charge
of a *Civil War*" (136). That Clarendon should have felt that much
of the religious controversy so prevelant in the seventeenth century
was a waste of time probably accounts for his disregard of such
disputes and possibly also for his failure to take the religious
scruples of others seriously. Clarendon's support of the Church of
England was tied to his view of the constitutional basis of the
monarchy. To attack the Church was to endanger the whole constitution, for "the ecclesiastical and civil state was so wrought and
interwoven together, and, in truth, so incorporated in each other,
that, like Hippocrates' twins, they cannot but laugh and cry
together" (4:40).

Chapter Eight
Clarendon: An Assessment

Clarendon's place in both English historiography and English literature rests upon his *History of the Rebellion and Civil Wars in England.* Although he wrote a large body of other work—essays, dialogues, meditations, pamphlets, speeches, letters—this material is primarily interesting today only to the extent to which it illustrates Clarendon's intellectual and political values. Yet had political circumstances been different—had there been, for example, no "rebellion" and no periods of exile—he probably would have written little to nothing.

To a very real extent all of his work, or very nearly all of it, was written in response to a "cause." He always was, in that sense, a propagandist, but he was a propagandist for what he believed. His was not a pen for hire. He began writing royalist pamphlets for the King in the early 1640s. When Clarendon fled from England with the Prince of Wales in the spring of 1646, he continued his efforts for the royalist cause by beginning the original "History." From the point at which he was forced to discontinue work on the "History" in 1648 until his banishment and exile in 1668, Clarendon wrote very little, only an occasional pamphlet in response to a particular propagandistic need. Once he had settled in exile, he returned to writing, beginning immediately a "Vindication" of himself from the specific charges of treason and then a "Life," a memoir of his political career. Finally, as we have seen, his reply to Hobbes's *Leviathan* and his books *Animadversions* and *Religion and Policy* also are responses to "causes," threats posed to the English constitution and monarchy by the "dangerous and pernicious" errors of a political philosophy articulated by Hobbes and by the possibility of Roman Catholicism being reestablished in England. From his very first efforts to his very last, Clarendon's works are defenses, vindications, interpretations. As the record of Clarendon's career as a writer shows, his major works all belong to either of the two periods of enforced exile—from 1646-48 or from 1668-74.

In many ways it can be argued that Clarendon's importance as historian is greater than his significance as a writer. The *History* and its manuscript materials represent one of the major primary sources of our knowledge of the political upheaval England experienced in the period from 1640 to 1660. Admittedly biased, often inaccurate, the *History* still contains information and insights which are unavailable elsewhere. As Sir Charles Firth has observed, the *History* is "the most valuable of all the contemporary accounts of the civil wars."[1] But it is difficult to assess in any way the impact that Clarendon's *History* had on later English historical works. For one thing, its publication was delayed. Although Clarendon finished the *History* in 1672, his position as an exiled, and disgraced minister precluded, in part, its immediate publication. Instead his sons Laurence and Henry waited until the accession of Queen Anne, Clarendon's granddaughter, to release the manuscript. When it was published in 1702-4, it was seen not simply for what it was, the first of the great English histories, but rather as a document of Tory propaganda. Its impact was political. James W. Thompson writes:

No one who has read the history of the reign of Queen Anne can have failed to observe the immense effect of the publication of Clarendon's work. It strengthened the convictions of a powerful section of the English public in the midst of balanced political struggle. As Clarendon's influence had formerly been great in the Restoration Settlement, so his *History of the Rebellion*, after its publication... continued his influence.... The Anglican Church received an enormous impulse, and the noble language which described the perils through which Church and State had lately passed fortified the constitution and left its mark upon the legislation of Queen Anne's reign.[2]

The reception which greeted the publication of the *History* was colored by the same partisanship which underlay its composition. It was attacked by John Oldmixon in, among other works, his *Clarendon and Whitlock Compar'd* (1727) as unfair and inaccurate and, later, as deceitfully edited. It was defended by John Burton in his *Genuineness of Ld Clarendon's History of the Rebellion Printed at Oxford Vindicated* (1744). Such disputes reveal much of the politics of the age in which they were written, but they say little about the lasting value of Clarendon's great *History*.

The *History* was once a popular book. It went through twenty editions from its first publication in 1702 until Macray's edition appeared in 1888. Today, the *History* is rarely read. The most that any student of literature is likely to encounter is a short selection, generally a "character" sketch, in an anthology of seventeenth-century writing. The reason is fairly simple and has nothing to do with Clarendon's *History*. One might similarly observe that few people read Gibbon or Macaulay. Literature is now a term applied almost exclusively to imaginative works; history is now a science rather than an art. What we have lost, as George Macaulay Trevelyan observed some seventy-five years ago, is the sense "that history was a part of the national literature, and was meant for the education and delight of all who read books."[3] Recognizing literary devices in the *History* can give us a new way of seeing and analyzing the narrative. Yet it does not suggest why a modern reader would be interested in Clarendon's work.

The answer is, in part, suggested by an observation made by Harold Nicolson: "Clarendon was the first to lay down the principle that history deals not only with facts but with human beings, that the problems of history are concerned primarily with human personality."[4] Personality pervades the *History* in two ways. Clarendon was unique in the tradition of English historical writing in that he wrote contemporary rather than retrospective history. He was both an actor and an interpreter. It is Clarendon's closeness to events and the men who shaped them that accounts for part of the *History*'s appeal. What sustains the *History* as a narrative work is Clarendon's voice. In many places the narrative is quite limited in its coverage. The *History*, after all, records events which occurred over a thirty-year period. There was much that Clarendon was forced to omit because he had no firsthand knowledge and no adequate source of information. Nevertheless, he wrote on, bridging the omissions with memoirlike privileged anecdotes of experiences. Consequently, it is this sense of the narrator which both holds the narrative together and compels our attention. As Leopold von Ranke has observed:

It is perfectly true, as has been said, that it is difficult to tear oneself away from the book, when once one is deep in it, especially the earlier sections; one converses with a living, intelligent, and powerful spirit.... The narrative is pervaded by a tone of honest conviction, which communicates itself to the reader. It is as if one were listening to a venerable gentleman narrating the events of his life in a circle of friends.[5]

Clarendon's interest in personality is also reflected in what is perhaps the most distinctive feature for which the *History* has been praised—its "character" sketches. To this end, he included in the *History* his assessments of the personalities of the major actors in his narrative. Writing as he was about his contemporaries, Clarendon conveys to the reader a sense of the individuals involved in a way that no modern historian could possibly achieve. Clarendon's assessments are personal and often biased. Nevertheless, we, as readers, accept his judgments. Through his "character" sketches we experience an immediacy and an illusion of reality.

Clarendon's *History of the Rebellion and Civil Wars in England* is a monumental work, one of the most important source books for the study of the seventeenth century. Clarendon played a vital role in one of the most crucial and complicated periods of England's history. His life and his works are a reflection of the England of the civil wars and the restoration. But, as I have been suggesting, the significance of Clarendon's *History* is tied to more than its scope, or its historical value; it is tied to his sense of personality which emerges from the work—the personality of both Clarendon himself and of the individual actors. What the *History* offers us, as the editors of a recent anthology have noted, is "one of the most engaging, penetrating, and enduring forms of literature: the comment of a man of integrity, wide views, deep experience, shrewdness, and passionate concern, and literary sophistication upon his fellows in a critical moment of history."[6]

Notes and References

Chapter One

1. Thomas H. Lister, *Life and Administration of Edward, First Earl of Clarendon* (London, 1838), 1: xvii.

2. Ibid., p. 63.

3. The speech is summarized by Lister, *Life*, 1:89-91. It was separately printed as *Mr. Hides Argument Before the Lords in the Upper House of Parliament. Aprill 1641* (n.p., 1641).

4. Summarized by Lister, *Life*, 1:80-86. Separately printed as *Mr. Edward Hyde's Speech at a Conference betweene both Houses...the 6th. of July, 1641. At the Transmission of the severall Impeachments against the Lord Chiefe Barron Davenport, Mr. Barron Trevor, and Mr. Barron Weston* (London, 1641).

5. B. H. G. Wormald, *Clarendon: Politics, History & Religion, 1640-1660* (Cambridge, 1951), p. 7.

6. Simonds D'Ewes, *The Journal of Sir Simonds D'Ewes from the First Recess of the Long Parliament to the Withdrawal of King Charles from London,* ed. Willson Havelock Coates (New Haven: Yale University Press, 1942), p. 45.

7. D'Ewes, *Journal*, pp. 94-95.

8. Published as *His Majesties Declaration, To all His Loving Subjects* (London, 1641) and printed in the *History* (4:168-72). An indispensable guide to Clarendon's propaganda efforts for the royalist cause is Graham Roebuck's *Clarendon and Cultural Continuity: A Bibliographical Study* (New York: Garland, 1981).

9. Wormald, *Clarendon*, p. 44.

10. S. R. Gardiner, *History of England from the Accession of James I. to the Outbreak of the Civil War* (London: Longmans, Green and Co., 1904), 10:169.

11. Ibid.

12. This piece was *Two Speeches Made in the House of Peeres, On Munday the 19th. of December, For, and Against Accommodation. The*

one by the Earle of Pembroke, the other by the Lord Brooke (n.p., 1642).
Hyde wrote both speeches.

13. After the failure of the treaty, Hyde published *Transcendent and Multiplied Rebellion and Treason, Discovered, by the Lawes of the Land* ([Oxford], 1645), a pamphlet defense of the king's position.

14. The extent and nature of Clarendon's reading during certain periods of his life can be established in great detail. MSS. Clarendon 126 and 127 include extensive notes and extracts from books which Clarendon read from 1635–73. *A Catalogue of a Collection of Manuscripts of the great Earl of Clarendon* ([London, 1764]) records other notes and extracts which presumably have been lost. The vast extent of his library can be seen from *Bibliotheca Clarendoniana: A Catalogue of the Valuable and Curious Library of ... Edward Earl of Clarendon* (1756).

15. Edward Hyde, *An Answer to a Pamphlet, Entit'led, A Declaration of the Commons of England in Parliament assembled, expressing their Reasons and Grounds of passing the late Resolutions touching no further Addresse or Application to be made to the King* (n.p., 1648).

16. Edward Hyde, *A Full Answer to an Infamous and Trayterous Pamphlet Entituled ...* (n.p., 1648).

17. Edward Hyde, *A Letter from a True and Lawful Member of Parliament, and One faithfully engaged with it, from the beginning of the War to the end* (n.p., 1656).

18. David Ogg, *England in the Reign of Charles II*, 2d ed. (London: Oxford University Press, 1956), 1:163.

19. Lister, *Life*, 2:36.

20. Quoted from J. P. Kenyon, ed., *The Stuart Constitution, 1603–168: Documents and Commentary* (Cambridge: Cambridge University Press, 1966), p. 358.

21. Ogg, *England*, 1: 202.

22. On Clarendon's part in and attitudes toward the religious settlement see R. S. Bosher, *The Making of the Restoration Settlement* (London, 1951) and George R. Abernathy, Jr., "Clarendon and the Declaration of Indulgence," *Journal of Ecclesiastical History* 11 (1960):55–73. Of particular relevance to Clarendon's attitudes in 1662-63 is his *Second Thoughts; or the Case of a Limited Toleration, Stated according to the present Exigence of Affairs in Church and State* ([London, 1663?]).

23. See, for example, the entry in Samuel Pepys's *Diary* for 22 February 1664.

24. Lister, *Life*, 2:135.

25. Entry for 20 February 1665.

26. Keith Feiling, *British Foreign Policy, 1660–1672* (1930; rpt. London: Frank Cass and Co., 1968), pp. 80, 81.

27. Entry for 14 June 1667.

28. As reported in John Milward, *The Diary of ... 1666–1668,* ed. Caroline Robbins (Cambridge: Cambridge University Press, 1938), p. 99.

29. The estimation is Pepys's—see the entry for 10 October 1666.

30. E. I. Carlyle, "Clarendon and the Privy Council, 1660–1667," *English Historical Review* 27 (1912):251, 253. Colonial administration under Clarendon is examined in Percy Lewis Kaye's *English Colonial Administration under Lord Clarendon, 1660–1667,* John Hopkins University Studies in Historical and Political Science, no. 23 (Baltimore, 1905).

31. Quoted in Henry Ellis, ed., *Original Letters*, 2d series (London: Harding and Lepard 1827), 4:39.

32. This was published first as a broadside *News from Dunkirk-House: Or, Clarendon's Farewell to England,* which is the same as *The Humble Petition and Address of Edward Earl of Clarendon.* A later, fuller reply was *The Petition and Address of the Right Honourable Edward, Late Earl of Clarendon, to the House of Lords; upon his withdrawing out of this Kingdom, towards the Close of the Year 1667* (London, 1715).

33. An account of the parliamentary proceedings against Clarendon is in *Cobbett's Complete Collection of State Trials* (London: R. Bagshaw, 1810), 6:293–511. See also Clayton Roberts, "The Impeachment of the Earl of Clarendon," *Cambridge Historical Journal* 13 (1957):1–18.

34. These were separately printed as *Two Letters Written by the Right Honourable Edward Earl of Clarendon, late Lord High Chancellour of England ...* (n.p., n.d.).

Chapter Two

1. Two manuscript copies of the original "History" survive. The first, now MS. Clarendon 112, is in Clarendon's handwriting. Clarendon used this manuscript when he worked the original "History" and the "Life" together. The second, now MS. Rawlinson D. 811, is a copy in the handwriting of two amanuases.

2. H.R. Trevor-Roper, "Clarendon and the Practice of History," in *Milton and Clarendon: Two Papers on 17th Century English Historiography* (Los Angeles, 1965), pp. 23–24.

3. Firth, "Clarendon's 'History,'" 1:34.

4. Ibid., 1:40.

5. Hyde did, apparently, begin writing Book V: "The fifth book.—wch is begun..." (MS. Clarendon 29, item 2406). This unpublished letter outlines Hyde's progress on the "History" in terms very similar to those in the letter to the Earl of Bristol (see *Clarendon State Papers*, 2:333-35). Part of the projected book might be MS. Clarendon 29, item 2383—some twenty pages of paragraphs on various related topics. This is dated from Jersey, October and December 1646.

6. Edward Hyde, *Transcendent and Multiplied Rebellion and Treason, Discovered, by the Lawes of the Land* ([Oxford], 1645).

7. There are two surviving copies of this manuscript. The first, the original in Clarendon's handwriting, is bound into the manuscript of the original "History" (MS. Clarendon 112). The second copy (MS. Clarendon 113) is in the handwriting of William Edgeman, Clarendon's secretary.

8. A copy of this in Clarendon's handwriting is in MS. Clarendon 112, where it begins on the bottom half of the last sheet of the "westerne businesse" manuscript. A second copy is in the handwriting of Edgeman (in MS. Clarendon 113). See preceding note.

9. Roy Pascal, *Design and Truth in Autobiography* (Cambridge, Mass.: Harvard University Press, 1960), p. 5.

10. The manuscript of the "Life," in Clarendon's handwriting, is MS. Clarendon 123. It was used by Clarendon in preparing the final *History*.

11. For example, see Wormald, *Clarendon*, pp. 3-4, 9-12.

12. Jean Le Clerc, *Mr. LeClerc's Account of the Earl of Clarendon's History of the Civil Wars,* tr. J.O., 2d ed. (London: Bernard Lintott, 1710), p. 4.

13. Firth, "Clarendon's 'History,'" 3: 464-65.

14. See C. V. Wedgwood, *Thomas Wentworth, First Earl of Strafford, 1593-1641: A Revaluation* (New York: Macmillan, 1962), pp. 316-17.

15. Firth, "Clarendon's 'History,'" 3: 470.

16. MSS. Clarendon 136 and 28, item 2226. Both are printed in Edward Walker's *Historical Discourses* (London: Sanuel Keble, 1705).

Chapter Three

1. MSS. Clarendon 126 and 127.

2. Peter Burke, *The Renaissance Sense of the Past* (London, 1969), p. 2.

3. Ibid., p. 7.

4. Ibid., p. 13.

5. Herschel Baker, *The Race of Time* (Toronto: University of Toronto Press, 1967), p. 16.

6. Quoted in J. R. Hale, ed., *The Evolution of British Historiography* (London, 1967), p. 12.

7. Herodotus's *History* recorded the struggle between the Persians and the Greeks from the time of Croesus (ca. 560 B.C.) to that of Xerxes (ca. 480 B.C.), a war which had ended in his childhood. Thucydides' *History of the Peloponnesian War* is a history of a war in which Thucydides had been a participant. Polybius's *History* traces the rise of Roman supremacy in the Mediterranean from the beginning of the first Punic War (264 B.C.) to the destruction of Carthage and Corinth (146 B.C.). Livy's history of the Roman people moves from the founding of the city to Livy's own time. Tacitus's *Histories* extend from the death of Nero (A.D.68) to the death of Domitian (A.D.96). His *Annals* are histories of the emperors from Tiberius (A.D.14) to Nero (A.D.68).

8. Tacitus, *Annals*, Book III:lxv, tr. Clifford H. Moore. Loeb Classical Library (Cambridge and London: Harvard University Press, 1931), 3:625.

9. Livy, *Ab Urbe Condita*, Preface to Book I, tr. B. O. Foster. Loeb Classical Library (Cambridge and London; Harvard University Press, 1925), 1:7.

10. F. Smith Fussner, *The Historical Revolution: English Historical Writing and Thought 1580-1640* (London, 1962), pp. 10-11.

11. Ibid., p. 13.

12. Machiavelli, *The Prince,* chapter 25, in Allan Gilbert, tr., *Machiavelli: The Chief Works and Others* (Durham, N.C.: Duke University Press, 1965), 1:89-90.

13. As quoted in Felix Raab, *The English Face of Machiavelli* (London, 1964), pp. 149-50.

14. H. C. Davila, *The Historie of the Civill Warres of France* (London, 1647), p. 2.

15. H. C. Davila, *The History of the Civil Wars of France* (London, 1678).

16. For another view of causation in Clarendon's *History* see Christopher Hill, "Lord Clarendon and the Puritan Revolution," in *Puritanism and Revolution* (New York, 1958), pp. 199-214.

17. Charles H. Firth, "Burnet as an Historian," in *Essays Historical and Literary* (Oxford, 1938), p. 207.

18. James Stephen, "Clarendon's 'History of the Rebellion,'" in *Horae Sabbaticae* (London: Macmillan,1892), 1:311.

19. All six were published in Charles E. H. Chadwyck Healey, ed., *Bellum Civile. Hopton's Narrative of his Campaign in the West (1642-1644) and other Papers.* Somerset Record Society, no. 18 (London: Harrison and Sons, 1902). The originals are MS. Clarendon 23, item 1738, nos. 1-4, 6, 7.

20. Firth, "Clarendon's 'History,'" 1:51.

21. MS. Clarendon 23, item 1751. Unpublished. Relevant sections in the *History* are 6:279-84.

22. MS. Clarendon 26, items 2062 and 2063. Unpublished.

23. MS. Clarendon 26, item 2074.

24. MS. Clarendon 31, item 2744. Unpublished.

25. MS. Clarendon 23, item 1805. Part of this—the last sheet only—is printed in Macray's edition of the *History* as a footnote to 8:75. Some additional notes for Books III to VIII appear in MS. Clarendon 36, item 331.

26. MSS. Clarendon 22, item 1669; 23, items 1764 and 1809. Each is endorsed by Hyde as "Sir Hugh Cholmeley's Memorials" and the last has been printed in *Clarendon State Papers*, 2:181-86.

27. MS. Clarendon 26, item 2064. Unpublished.

28. MS. Clarendon 23, item 1738, no. 5. Portions of it have been published in Walter Money's *The First and Second Battles of Newbury*, 2d ed. (London: Simpkin, Marshall, and Co., 1884). The original manuscript is dated from St. Germains on 10 December 1647.

29. MS. Clarendon 23, item 1738, no. 8.

30. MS. Clarendon 28, item 2254. Published by Charles H. Firth, "The Journal of Prince Rupert's Marches, 5 Sept. 1642 to 4 July 1646," *English Historical Review* 13 (1898): 729-41.

31. MSS. Clarendon 136 and 28, item 2226. Both are printed in Walker's *Historical Discourses*.

32. Firth, "Clarendon's 'History,'" 1:51.

33. Hyde's attempts can be seen in letters to Lord Widdrington, 5 August 1646; to Dr. John Earle, 1 January 1646 (both in *Clarendon State Papers*, 2:246, 322); to Earle again, 12 February 1647 (MS. Clarendon 29, item 2442); and finally to Earle 16 March 1647 (*Clarendon State Papers*, 2: 350).

34. MS. Clarendon 34, item 2978.

35. William Edgeman, Clarendon's secretary, kept a record of the embassy: "Journal of the Embassy into Spain." It covers the period from 27 May 1649 to 11 November 1654. It is now MS. Clarendon 137.

36. The sections are 9:175-77 and 10:23-32. This material is in the Clarendon MSS. The letters which passed between the two are printed in *Clarendon State Papers*, 2:209-25.

37. Firth, "Clarendon's 'History,'" 3:477.

38. Langdale's account is MS. Clarendon 31, item 2862; Musgrave's is MS. Clarendon 31, item 2867.

39. A full description of all this material can be found in the *Calender of the Clarendon State Papers,* ed O. Ogle and W. H. Bliss (Oxford, 1872), 1:443–44, 447–58. It is all collected in MSS. Clarendon 32 and 33.

40. Firth, "Clarendon's 'History,'" 3:482.

Chapter Four

1. G. M. Trevelyan, *Clio, A Muse and Other Essays* (London: Longmans, Green and Co., 1914), pp. 1, 2, 36.

2. The title of Hayden White's article in *The Writing of History,* ed. Robert H. Canary and Henry Kozicki (Madison: University of Wisconsin Press, 1978), pp. 41–62.

3. Ibid., p. 42.

4. Ibid., p. 47.

5. Hayden White, *Metahistory* (Baltimore: The John Hopkins University Press, 1973), p. 7.

6. Throughout this chapter I have used the definitions in C. Hugh Holman et al. *A Handbook of Literature,* 4th ed. (New York: Odyssey, 1979), in my discussions of plot, character, and narrative voice.

7. White, "Historical Text," p. 48.

8. Ibid., pp. 49-50.

9. White, *Metahistory,* p. 8.

10. Ibid.

11. White, "Historical Text," p. 52.

12. E. M. W. Tillyard, *The English Epic and Its Background* (London: Chatto and Windus, 1954), p. 450.

13. Letter to Samuel Pepys, 20 January 1703. Reprinted in *Memoirs of Samuel Pepys,* ed. Richard, Lord Braybrooke (London: Henry Colburn, 1828), 5:437.

14. Philip A. Knachel, ed., *Eikon Basilike* (Ithaca: Folger Shakespeare Library, 1966), pp. xiii, xiv.

Chapter Five

1. Letter dated 12 August 1689. A description and history of the gallery can be found in Lady Theresa Lewis, *Lives of the Friends and Contemporaries of Lord Chancellor Clarendon,* 3 vols. (London: John Murray, 1852).

2. See, for example, David Nicol Smith, *Characters from the Histories and Memoirs of the Seventeenth Century* (Oxford, 1918), p. xviii.

3. MSS. Clarendon 126 and 127.

4. Cicero, *De Oratore*, Book II: xv, tr. E. W. Sutton and H. Rackham. Loeb Classical Library, rev. ed. (Cambridge and London:Harvard University Press, 1948), 3:245.

5. Thucydides, *History*, Book I:xxii, tr. Charles Forster Smith. Loeb Classical Library, rev. ed. (Cambridge and London: Harvard University Press, 1928), 1:41.

6. Tacitus, *Annals*, Book III:lxv, tr. Clifford H. Moore. Loeb Classical Library, 3:625.

7. Livy, *Ab Urbe Condita*, Preface to Book I, tr. B. O. Foster. Loeb Classical Library, 1:7.

8. Alan Wardman, *Plutarch's "Lives"* (Berkeley: University of California Press, 1974), p. 105.

9. *Theophrastus: The Character Sketches*, tr. Warren Anderson (Kent, Ohio: Kent State University Press, 1970), p. 73.

10. John Hall, *Character Writings of the Seventeenth Century*, ed. Henry Morley (London: George Routledge and Sons, 1891), p. 109. This is a convenient collection of seventeenth-century characters.

11. Benjamin Boyce, *The Theophrastan Character in England to 1642* (Cambridge, Mass.: Harvard University Press, 1947), p. 143.

12. Ibid., p. 247.

13. Firth, "Clarendon's 'History'" 2:253.

14. Letter to Samuel Pepys, 20 January 1703. Reprinted in *Memoirs of Samuel Pepys*, ed. Richard, Lord Braybrooke (London, 1828), 5:437.

15. The original is taken from *In Catilinam*, 3:16.

16. Proof that Clarendon did use the character as a way of dealing with his own fall from power can also be seen in three sketches of men who had actively worked against him—the Earl of Bristol, Lord Berkeley, and Lord Arlington. Composed in April 1669, just after he completed part one of the "Life," these characters do not appear in the *History*; they are printed in *Clarendon State Papers*, 3, supplement, pp. 1i-1xxxiv.

17. The character is conveniently reprinted in Smith, *Characters*, pp. 227-29, from which text this quotation is taken.

Chapter Six

1. Significant portions are conveniently reprinted in Kenyon, *Stuart*, pp. 12-14.

2. Sir Charles Firth, "Hyde, Edward, First Earl of Clarendon," *DNB* (1891-92),10:377.

3. John Bowle, *Hobbes and His Critics* (London, 1969), p. 157.

4. Erasmus, *The Education of a Christian Prince*, ed. and tr. Lester K. Born (New York: Columbia University Press, 1936), p. 159.

5. As quoted in *Elizabethan Backgrounds*, ed. Arthur F. Kinney (Hamden, Conn.: Archon, 1975), pp. 60-61.

6. J. G. A. Pocock, *The Ancient Constitution and the Feudal Law* (Cambridge, 1957), p. 17.

7. Kenyon, *Stuart*, p. 7.

8. Raab, *Machiavelli*, p. 1.

9. Machiavelli, *The Prince*, ed. and tr. Robert M. Adams (New York: Norton, 1977), chapter 15.

10. Ernst Cassirer, *The Myth of the State* (New Haven: Yale University Press, 1946), p., 150.

11. Machiavelli, *Prince*, chapter 15.

12. *The Discourses of Niccolò Machiavelli*, ed. and tr. Leslie J. Walker (New Haven, 1950), 1:Book I, Discourse 11.

13. As quoted in Raab, *Machiavelli*, pp. 149-50.

14. The classic study of the theory is that of John Nevill Figgis, *The Divine Right of Kings*, 2d ed. (Cambridge: Cambridge University Press, 1914).

15. David Harris Willson, *King James VI and I* (London: Jonathan Cape, 1956), p. 132.

16. Conveniently reprinted in part in Kenyon, *Stuart*, pp. 12-14.

17. From "The King's Answer to the Nineteen Propositions, 18 June 1642," ibid., pp. 21-23.

18. Clarendon's views are discussed in his *Life* (Oxford, 1857), 2:61-62.

19. Corinne C. Weston, "The Theory of Mixed Monarchy under Charles I and After," *English Historical Review* 75 (1960):433.

20. Thomas Hobbes, *Behemoth or The Long Parliament*, ed. Ferdinand Tönnies, 2d ed. (1889; rpt. London: Frank Cass and Co.,1969), pp. 114-15.

21. Thomas Hobbes, *Leviathan*, p. 186. All quotations from *Leviathan* in the text are to the Penguin paperback edition (London, 1968), which reprints the *Head* edition printed for Andrew Crooke (London, 1651).

22. Ibid., p. 190.

23. Ibid., p. 120.

24. Ibid., p. 415.

25. Ibid., p. 504.

26. Ibid., pp. 498, 499.

27. Printed in Peter Barwick, *The Life of the Reverend Dr. John Barwick* (London: J. Bettenham, 1724), p. 430.

28. There is a full checklist of "anti-Hobbes literature and allusion" in Samuel I. Mintz, *The Hunting of Leviathan: Seventeenth-Century Reactions to the Materialism and Moral Philosophy of Thomas Hobbes* (Cambridge: Cambridge University Press, 1969), pp. 157–60.

29. Bowle, *Hobbes*, p. 167.

30. Hobbes, *Leviathan*, p. 527.

Chapter Seven

1. See J. N. Figgis, "Erastus and Erastianism," *Journal of Theological Studies* 2(1900):66–101.

2. Stephen Neill, *Anglicanism*, 3d ed. (Baltimore: Penguin, 1965), p. 107.

3. A. O. Meyer, *England and the Catholic Church under Queen Elizabeth*, tr. J. R. McKee (1914; rpt. New York: Barnes and Noble, 1967), p. 85.

4. William Cecil, *The Execution of Justice in England*, ed. Robert M. Kingdon (Ithaca: Folger Shakespeare Library, 1965), p. 15.

5. As reprinted in Kenyon, *Stuart*, pp. 231–32.

6. John Miller, *Popery and Politics in England, 1660–1688* (Cambridge: Cambridge University Press, 1973), p. 85. My discussion in these sections is indebted in places to Miller's book.

7. Ibid., p. 93.

8. The best guide to Chillingworth's theology is Robert R. Orr, *Reason and Authority: The Thought of William Chillingworth* (Oxford: Clarendon Press, 1967).

9. There is a good summary in Wormald, *Clarendon*, pp. 244–61.

10. Anthony à Wood, *Athenae Oxonienses*, ed. Philip Bliss, 3d ed. (1817; rpt. Hildesheim: G. Olms, 1969), 3:col. 1014.

11. Edward Stillingfleet, *A Discourse*. There were three editions of this in 1672. Subsequent quotations are from the second edition (London, 1672).

12. Hugh Paulinus Cressy, *Fanaticism Fanatically Imputed* (n. p., 1672).

13. Stillingfleet's reply was contained in *An Answer to several late Treatises*, 2 pts. (London, 1673). Clarendon's *Animadversions* was published in London in 1673. The fifth and sixth titles in the exchange were

Cressy's apology, *An Epistle Apologetical of S. Cressy to a Person of Honour* [Clarendon], *touching his vindication of Dr. Stillingfleet* (London, 1674), and Stillingfleet's *An Answer to Mr. Cressy's Epistle Apologetical* (London, 1675).

14. Stillingfleet, *Discourse*, p. 209.

15. Ibid., p. 298.

16. Cressy, *Fanaticism*, pp. 89, 92.

17. Stillingfleet, *Discourse*, p. 490.

18. The list of Popes is MS. Clarendon 140; the notes from the Bullarium are in MS. Clarendon 126.

19. MS. Clarendon 125, paginated by Shaw, 1–407. *Religion and Policy* was not published until 1811.

20. Meyer, *England*, pp. 269ff.

Chapter Eight

1. Charles H. Firth, "Hyde, Edward, First Earl of Clarendon," *DNB* (1891–92), 10:386.

2. James W. Thompson, *A History of Historical Writing* (New York: Macmillan, 1942), 1:643–44.

3. Trevelyan, *Clio*, p. 36.

4. Harold Nicolson, *The Development of English Biography* (London: Hogarth Press, 1968), p. 44.

5. Leopold von Ranke, *A History of England Principally in the Seventeenth Century* (Oxford, 1875), 6:28–29.

6. Helen White, Ruth C. Wallerstein, and Ricardo Quintana, eds., *Seventeenth-Century Verse and Prose* (New York: Macmillan, 1951), 2:23.

Selected Bibliography

PRIMARY SOURCES

Animadversions Upon a Book, Intituled; Fanaticism Fanatically Imputed to the Catholick Church, by Dr. Stillingfleet, and the Imputation Refuted and Retorted by S[erenus] *C*[ressy]. London: R. Royston, 1673.

A Brief View and Survey of the Dangerous and pernicious Errors to Church and State, in Mr. Hobbes's Book, Entitled Leviathan. Oxford, 1676.

A Compleat Collection of Tracts. London: C. Davis, 1747. (Cited as *Tracts.*) Includes, among others, "Relections upon Several Christian Duties, Divine and Moral, by Way of Essays" and "Contemplations and Reflexions upon the Psalms of David."

The History of the Rebellion and Civil Wars in England. Edited by W. Dunn Macray. 6 vols. Oxford: Clarendon Press, 1888.

The Life of Edward Earl of Clarendon...in which is included, A Continuation of his History of the Grand Rebellion. (Cited as *Life.*) 2 vols. Oxford: Oxford University Press, 1857.

Religion and Policy and the Countenance and Assistance Each Should Give to the Other. With a Survey of the Power and Jurisdiction of the Pope in the Dominions of other Princes. 2 vols. Oxford: Clarendon Press, 1811.

State Papers Collected by Edward, Earl of Clarendon. 3 vols. Oxford: Clarendon Press, 1767–86. (Cited as *Clarendon State Papers.*)

SECONDARY SOURCES

1. Principal Works Concerned with Clarendon's Life and Writings.

Abernathy, George R., Jr. "Clarendon and the Declaration of Indulgence." *Journal of Ecclesiastical History* 11(1960):55–73. Clarendon's part in the Restoration religious settlement. See next item as well.

Bosher, Robert S. *The Making of the Restoration Settlement: The Influence of the Laudians, 1649-1662.* London: Dacre Press, 1951. Restoration religious settlement. See also previous item for another view.

Bowle, John. *Hobbes and his Critics: A Study in Seventeenth Century Constitutionalism.* 1951; rpt. London: Frank Cass, 1969. Has a chapter on Clarendon's *A Brief View.*

Braudy, Leo. *Narrative Form in History and Fiction.* Princeton: Princeton University Press, 1970. Brief mention of Clarendon, pp. 14-21.

Carlyle, Edward I. "Clarendon and the Privy Council, 1660-1667." *English Historical Review* 27(1912):251-73. Administration of government under Clarendon.

Coltman, Irene. *Private Men and Public Causes: Philosophy and Politics in the English Civil War.* London: Faber and Faber, 1962. Three essays on "Clarendon and the Country," "Clarendon and Conscience," and "Clarendon and Cicero," each of which turns about the problems of "political consent."

Craik, Henry. *The Life of Edward Earl of Clarendon.* 2 vols. London: Smith, Elder, 1911. Appreciative but not as valuable as Lister, cited below.

Feiling, Keith. *A History of the Tory Party, 1640-1714.* Oxford: Clarendon Press, 1924. Standard. Chapter 5 deals with Clarendon's administration under Charles II.

Firth, Charles H. "Clarendon's 'History of the Rebellion.'" *English Historical Review* 19(1904):26-54, 245-62, 464-83. (Cited as Firth, 1, 2, or 3.) Detailed study of the three stages of the *History.*

———. "Edward Hyde, Earl of Clarendon, as Statesman, Historian, and Chancellor of the University." Reprinted in *Essays Historical and Literary.* Oxford: Clarendon Press, 1938, pp. 103-28. Text of a lecture delivered in 1909.

———. "Hyde, Edward, First Earl of Clarendon." In *Dictionary of National Biography.* Oxford: Oxford University Press, 1911, 10: 370-89. Brief biography and bibliography.

Hardacre, P. H. "Portrait of a Bibliophile: Edward Hyde, Earl of Clarendon, 1609-74." *Book Collector* 7(1958):361-68. The nature and extent of Clarendon's library.

Hill, Christopher. "Lord Clarendon and the Puritan Revolution." In *Puritanism and Revolution.* New York: Schocken Books, 1958, pp. 199-214. A perceptive general study.

Huehns, G., ed. *Clarendon: Selections from "The History of the Rebellion and Civil Wars" and "The Life by Himself."* Oxford: Oxford University Press, 1955. Substantial selections with a good introduction.

Kaye, Percy Lewis. *English Colonial Administration under Lord Clarendon, 1660-1667.* Johns Hopkins University Studies in Historical and Political Science, no. 23. Baltimore: The Johns Hopkins Press, 1905.

Knights, L. C. "Reflections on Clarendon's *History of the Rebellion.*" Reprinted in *Further Explorations.* Stanford: Stanford University Press, 1965, pp. 121-37. Text of a lecture stressing the "value" of the *History.*

Lee, Maurice, Jr. "The End of Clarendon." In *The Cabel.* Urbana: University of Illinois Press, 1965, pp. 1-27. Clarendon's fall from power.

Lister, Thomas H. *Life and Administration of Edward, First Earl of Clarendon.* 3 vols. London: Longman, 1838. Still the best biography. The third volume is composed of letters and papers from the Clarendon MSS. at the Bodleian Library, Oxford.

Ogle, O., Bliss, W. H., Macray, W. D., and Routledge, F. J., eds. *Calender of the Clarendon State Papers in the Bodleian Library.* 5 vols. Oxford: Clarendon Press, 1876-1970. Itemized contents of the Clarendon State Papers manuscripts.

Raab, Felix. *The English Face of Machiavelli.* London: Routledge and Kegan Paul, 1964. Some suggestive comments on the influence of Machiavelli on Clarendon's thought, pp. 146-53.

Ranke, Leopold Von. *A History of England Principally in the Seventeenth Century.* 6 vols. Oxford: Clarendon Press, 1875. Remarks on Clarendon's *History*, 6:3-29.

Roberts, Clayton. "The Impeachment of the Earl of Clarendon." *Cambridge Historical Journal* 13(1957):1-18. The best account.

Roebuck, Graham. *Clarendon and Cultural Continuity.* New York: Garland, 1981. Comprehensive description of works by and about Clarendon.

Rowse, A. L. "Clarendon's Life." In *The English Spirit: Essays in History and Literature.* New York: Macmillan, 1945, pp. 169-75. Short appreciative essay.

Smith, David Nichol. *Characters from the Histories and Memoirs of the Seventeenth Century.* Oxford: Clarendon Press, 1918. Anthology with a generous selection of Clarendon's character sketches from the *History* and *Life* and a good introduction.

Trevor-Roper, H. R. "Clarendon and the Great Rebellion." In *Historical Essays*. London: Macmillan, 1957; rpt. New York: Harper and Row, 1966, pp. 244–48. Short appreciative essay.

_____ "Clarendon and the Practice of History." In *Milton and Clarendon: Two Papers on 17th Century English Historiography*. Los Angeles: William Andrews Clark Memorial Library, 1965, pp. 21–50. Text of a lecture.

Underdown, David. *Royalist Conspiracy in England, 1649–1660*. New Haven: Yale University Press, 1960. Helpful on Clarendon's relationship to royalist plans within England.

Ward, A. W. and Waller, A. R., eds. *The Cambridge History of English Literature*. 15 vols. Cambridge: University Press, 1907–27. A. W. Ward discusses Clarendon, 7:241–51.

Watson, George. "The Reader in Clarendon's *History of the Rebellion*." *RES*, N.S. 25 (1974):396–409. Deals with the intended audience for whom the *History* was written.

Wedgwood, C. V. "Some Contemporary Accounts of the Great Civil War." *Transactions of the Royal Society of Literature* 26 (1953):71–88. Some suggestive comparisons.

Wormald, B. H. G. *Clarendon: Politics, History and Religion, 1640–1660*. Cambridge: Cambridge University Press, 1951. The standard study within the chronological limits indicated in the title.

2. Useful Background Material

Although the following items contain little or no discussion of Clarendon's work, they are valuable for providing the larger background against which independent judgments can be made.

Burke, Peter. *The Renaissance Sense of the Past*. London: Edward Arnold, 1969. A good general introduction to Renaissance historiography.

Delany, Paul. *British Autobiography in the Seventeenth Century*. New York: Columbia University Press, 1969. The best survey.

Fussner, F. Smith. *The Historical Revolution: English Historical Writing and Thought, 1580–1640*. London: Routledge and Kegan Paul, 1962. A valuable overview of the "types" of history.

Hale, J. R., ed. *The Evolution of British Historiography: From Bacon to Namier*. London: Macmillan, 1967. Largely an anthology but a long introductory essay.

Pocock, J. G. A.   *The Ancient Constitution and the Feudal Law: English Historical Thought in the Seventeenth Century.* Cambridge: Cambridge University Press, 1957. Relationship between law and history.

Zagorin, Perez.   *A History of Political Thought in the English Revolution.* London: Routledge and Kegan Paul, 1954. Standard survey.

Index